VISITORS WHO NEVER LEFT

Visitors Who Never Left

The Origin of the People of
Damelahamid

Translated and arranged by

CHIEF KENNETH B. HARRIS

in collaboration with

FRANCES M. P. ROBINSON
Department of Fine Arts, University of
British Columbia

UNIVERSITY OF BRITISH COLUMBIA PRESS

VISITORS WHO NEVER LEFT

The Origin of the People of Damelahamid

Canadian Shared Cataloguing in Publication Data
Visitors who never left: the origin of the people of Damelahamid.
Translated by Ken B. Harris in collaboration with Frances
M. P. Robinson.

1. Gitshian Indians — Legends. I. Harris, Ken B., tr. II.
Robinson, Frances M. P.
E 99 G58 V58   970.3

International Standard Book Number
(Hardcover edition) 0-7748-0033-X
(Paperback edition) 0-7748-0034-8

Printed in Canada

For Irene Harris

Tsim ham haemid
Goemessnech
Hiswildoget

c 1888-1972.

CANADA

I am delighted to extend my warmest congratulations to Chief Ken Harris, on the occasion of the publication of <u>Visitors Who Never Left</u>.

This highly important event enables many people to share the wisdom, mystery and memory of the people of the Damelahamid. Through such sharing, we are immeasurably enriched and we are more fully appreciative of the quality and the depth of our Canadian heritage.

May <u>Hagbegwatku</u> continue to bring understanding and goodwill to the world.

Pierre Elliott Trudeau

Ottawa,
1 9 7 4.

Contents

Introduction

This project began in May 1969 when I first met Ken Harris in Prince Rupert, B.C., and he mentioned to me that he had in his possession some seven audiotapes relating the ancient stories of his people. It took more than two years for me to become acquainted with the Harris family and familiar with the region known as *Damelahamid*. It was another two years before the laborious process of translating the tapes was accomplished.

These, then, are the myths of *Damelahamid*,[1] a utopian paradise, lying between the Nass and Skeena Rivers in northern British Columbia. According to these stories, the earliest inhabitants came to earth from Heaven and brought the unenlightened Indian people then living in surrounding areas their culture. Many descendants still live in the ancient area bounded by the villages of Kispiox, Kitwancool, Kitwanga, and Kitsegucla.

These people are known as Gitshian, or Gitksan, and, as Ken Harris's stories show, still do not consider themselves part of the Tsimshian group in which anthropologists place them. Boas says that it seems probable that the Tsimshian first lived on the upper Skeena River,[2] and Garfield describes the areas of the Tsimshian as encompassing both the Nass and Skeena River valleys, ranging from Portland Canal in the north to Swindle Island in the south on the coast, with the Haida of the Queen Charlotte Islands in the Pacific their westernmost neighbours.[3] The Tlingit live in the north, and the Kwakiutl, Bella Bella, and Bella Coola, in the south. Inland, the eastern boundary is formed by Athapascan-speaking peoples. According to Ken Harris, in ancient times the Pacific Ocean is believed to have lapped the shores of *Damelahamid* before receding to its present position.

The character of the Indians in the myths is inextricably part of the land itself. The waters of the Nass and Skeena Rivers are strong and

---

[1] Note the various spellings for *Damelahamid*. Barbeau — *Temlaham*; Boas — *T!Em-lax-ā'm*; Robinson — *Tum-L-Hama*.

[2] Franz Boas, *Tsimshian Mythology* (Washington, D.C.: Government Printing Office, 1916), p. 483.

[3] Viola E. Garfield, *The Tsimshian Indians and their Arts* (Seattle: University of Washington Press, 1950), p. 5.

relentless; the mountain ranges are impassive and heavy. The immense mass of stone, Mt. Rocher Deboule or *Stekyawden*, broods over the lush valley. Everywhere there is colour. The mountains change from greys to greens to purples as days gather into seasons. The green valleys become gold and bronze in the autumn from the changing alders, birches, cottonwood, maples, and willows. The slow-moving, mighty ribbons of water mirror the greys and blues and whites of the sky. The Skeena is known as "The River of the Mists." Both rivers flatten at their mouths, wrapping themselves around many small islands before sweeping out to become lost in the Pacific. The mists along the lower reaches of the rivers are reluctant to rise and act as a sound muffler. Much of the area has remained unchanged over the centuries. Cedars, red and yellow, fir, spruce, and hemlock grow on the mountainsides. The Indians can travel in their canoes about eighty miles up the Nass River and almost two hundred and fifty miles up the Skeena.

In order to appreciate the significance of myths in the lives of these people, it is important to understand their everyday lives and their culture. The ancient Tsimshians were a migratory people who lived and hunted in the land bounded by the Nass and the Skeena. They fished in these waters and along the coast of the Pacific. The movements of animals and fish and the harvesting of berries dictated their migrations. Wild life still exists in profusion — bear, moose, mountain goats, many different kinds of salmon.

Two elements of Tsimshian culture differentiate these people from their neighbours. Their language is distinct, divided into three mutually intelligible dialects. Niska is spoken on the Nass; Coast Tsimshian on the lower Skeena, and Gitksan on the upper Skeena. Also, the Tsimshian have four phratries made up of four exogamous kinship divisions — Eagle, Wolf, Frog, and Fireweed. The Tlingit and the Haida, whose myths most closely resemble those of the Tsimshian, each have two. All three people have complex, matrilineal clan organizations.

Garfield points out that:

> Phratries had no important function other than the regulation of spouse selection. They were essentially loose federations of clans, which were the named subdivisions of phratries. Each clan included people who shared legends, a history of common ancestors, and many crests, properties and privileges. The members of some clans within a phratry had little in common with other clans of the same phratry except the fact that they could not intermarry.[4]

[4] Ibid., p. 20.

In such a matrilineal system, a boy belonged to his mother's clan and inherited his names, his position of rank, the traditions of songs, stories and crests, from his mother's brother, his uncle, not his father. Since the children belonged to their mother's kinship group, they automatically were members of her clan and her phratry.

Boas felt that class prejudice was very strong among the Tsimshian because all marriages had to take place among members of the same social rank. But more importantly, marriages were contractual agreements between lineages, demonstrating political ties and the maintenance of wealth and social position. Rank was maintained by displays of wealth and by ingrained systems of inheritance and kinship. Kinship groups had rights to certain economic privileges such as the ownership of salmon streams and various berry patches. Other closely guarded sources of wealth were the exclusive ownership of important names, songs, laments, dances, ceremonies, crests and myths. Members of a clan shared common traditions and followed strict laws of inheritance.

There were heads of clans and their families forming a "nobility." Other people fell into the "commoner" class. There was also a permanent class of slaves formed from members captured from outside groups. Servants, usually poor people regarded as part of a chief's household, were from the "commoner" class and were distinct from slaves. They did not have titles but were given amusing and unimportant names such as "semen."[5] They were faithful retainers, born in the village and part of the system. Those in slavery lost all familial, lineage, clan, and phratric affiliations. Their children were also slaves, and their owners had absolute power over them. According to Garfield, slaves were the most expensive potlatch gifts, with their monetary value in the nineteenth century ranging up to one thousand dollars each.

Tsimshian homes were built of cedar, usually rectangular in shape, some being excavated and others having a flat earth floor. The head of the house and his family lived in the central space at the back of the house. Close male relatives lived on either side of him, and slaves slept on either side of the entrance. The cooking fire was in the centre of the house, with firewood, heating stones, wooden storage and cooking boxes, tongs, and dishes nearby. The Indians slept on a raised platform running around the interior of the house. According to some descriptions this platform was not continuous but "broken" or divided into different family areas. Separate huts were sometimes built for menstruant women, or existing caves were enlarged for them. Another practice was to place adolescent

[5] Personal communication with the author.

girls in an enclosure behind a screen placed at the back of the house. Great care was taken in the education of children. For the daughters of chiefs, chastity was a prime virtue. These girls slept on raised platforms, the access to which was by means of a ladder at the foot of which a slave woman slept.

The most important food source for the Tsimshian was salmon. Oola-chen, a fish running up the Nass River, provided a vital source of oil and fat. Cod, halibut, herring, shellfish, seaweed, barnacles, and chitons, as well as seals, sea-lions, and otters, were harvested from the sea and shore. Shoots, roots, barks, and berries were gathered in season. Hunting for animals and birds was usually a fall occupation. All the productive shores and lands were apportioned to various clans.

There was a strong belief in guardian spirit powers. Spirit power acquisition and protection was for those who followed prescribed "purification" rites of ritual bathing, fasting, purgative-taking, sexual continence, and periods of solitude. Before a hunting trip the men followed these rules. Continence of both the men and their wives was very important, and breaking this rule meant ill luck to either or both parties. A menstruant woman's contact was also dangerous, and thus she was segregated.

The position women occupied in Tsimshian society is interesting. Their importance in the maintenance of class and rank was clearly recognized in allowing them into secret societies and by giving them hereditary dancing powers belonging to their lineages. They could also become shamans and compose songs for feasts.

Just as the matrilinial system was binding among the Tsimshian, they lived according to laws which had their origin in ancient times and which were handed down to succeeding generations via myths, chants, and laments. The Tsimshian, among other Northwest Coast people, also erected totem poles. In the following collection, one of the myths explains the origin of the totem pole. According to Ken Harris, the first was a gift to the people of *Damelahamid* from their Father-in-Heaven. Today, there are old totem poles in the villages, tucked away in valleys far from the main roads, standing, watching, waiting, guarding their secrets. Here, twentieth-century time is meaningless.

Time also appears warped in the myths themselves. Elements appear out of sequence. This is understandable as myths are a mixture of purely fictitious narrative usually involving supernatural persons, actions, and events, and popular ideas concerning both natural and historical phenomena. As such, all discrepancies are acceptable. Myths should not be tampered with. They belong to the people for whom they are meaningful as they stand. Over the years there are bound to be both additions and omissions. The old story-tellers and guardians of the myths tried to keep the flow of events pure and untainted, and what appear as irrelevancies are probably important and integral parts of a myth's structure.

Myths cannot be separated from actuality. They serve many purposes and are part of the total culture. They have many meanings and operate on several different levels of meaning. What might be difficult to acknowledge openly, such as immoral behaviour, can be handled satisfactorily by myth. There are often many versions of one myth, and every version can be authentic and therefore relevant.

The foregoing has been both a general background to the Tsimshian people and to the meaning of myths. It is now important to examine in greater detail myth *per se*.

Oral mythology represents the logical process of reasoning in the mind of a person from a culture which does not have the paradigm of scientific rationality. Oral traditions are logically reasoned explanations for phenomena for which there is no immediate understanding. There is no reason why logical reasoning without the benefit of scientific empirical rationality should be given less credence than empirical rational thought processes because, in essence, both are the attempts of human beings to reason logically. What may appear to be psychic phenomena in one culture may be understood to be logical truth in another.

Claude Levi-Strauss defines four levels for myth analysis: economic-technological, geographical, sociological, and cosmological. One should perhaps seek the logic of oral traditions in the cosmological aspects of Ken Harris's myths. On the three remaining levels, technological data, place names, and social data provide home-spun regional and cultural familiarity for the myths' audience.

As long as the oral traditions are maintained faithfully, there is every reason to expect the logical truths to pass more or less intact from one generation to the next. When modifications to the original logic arise, one might try to seek evidence of extrinsic change in or upon the cultural group in question. For example, when contact with the white man is established, a new set of problems arises and requires a logical cultural explanation to restore the world to order. Hence old myths are altered, or new ones are generated, to explain the process of culture change.

Because myths are repeated in separate cultures but with differing details, the stories collected by Boas, Swanton and, later, Robinson, have been referred to in the following collection. Franz Boas was the first empirical field-worker to arrive on the Northwest Coast to study Indian culture. Swanton and others followed in the Boas tradition of field work.

It is important to be aware of the changes that have occurred in the myth corpora since the turn of the century. The myths related by Ken Harris appear to contain far less detail than the earlier ones. The logical elements remain the same, and, it might be argued, less detail is needed today in the current cultural context to convey these same logical truths.

Analysis of similarities between the oral literature of the Tsimshian and that of their neighbours, reveals closest affinities with the Tlingit and the Haida. Plots, themes, and independent motifs are woven into dissimilar but recognizable tales.

In the oral tradition, the audience played an important role in the telling of the myth by ensuring that important details in the story were not changed or neglected. When a discrepancy occurred, the myth had to be retold correctly. As audiences became smaller, and those members of the audience who knew the correct versions of the myth in their entirety also declined in number, the details of the myth suffered. This collection is therefore important, even though Ken Harris was translating and then speaking onto a tape, because it might well be one of the last instances in which this body of myths could be told from personal memory.

Customs as well as values are set down by tradition, and once established, they become important to the smooth working of a society. It will be seen, therefore, that myths have meaning and function for the society of their origin. They may be equated to a guide-book for successful living within the culturally-defined bounds of the society. Customs and values are built out of past experience and belief. Myths describe the customs, define values, and set the barometer for acceptable patterns of living in a particular culture. Ken Harris considers them as lessons in the ethics of living, and also as definitions of family relationships. They play an extremely important part in the hereditary rights system. They are significant in establishing the rights of any one family to particular titles and crests and to geographical areas. At large gatherings, the right to those certain titles would be extolled and reinforced, and public recognition of that right solicited. The occasion would be supported by myths and, in turn, become part of those myths. Thus, the oral literature reflects the complexity of the development of Tsimshian lineages, clans, and villages.

The Indians believe that all the myths were indeed of "happenings in history." As all experiences related from earlier times are preserved in a pattern of myth-age adventures, a separation of myth from historical fact is for the most part impossible. There is no clear-cut distinction between the events of this world and those of other worlds. Further complexity results from the lack of cohesion between episodes and plots, a feature which arises because episodes and motifs can be combined in many ways. But the apparent confusion is not felt by the Indian. As Ken Harris puts it, "White people make things so complicated. Indians have evolved a simple way of looking at the world and of living."

As has been noted, myths are didactic in nature. If any of the commandments from the Father-in-Heaven — such as the honouring of animals — was broken, punishment was swift and severe. Indeed, beliefs relating to the immortality of certain animals and fish were universal throughout the Northwest Coast. Animals came from a race of supernatural beings and could assume certain forms. They were always to be ceremoniously and courteously handled. A break with this tradition led to disaster. Frogs, killer whales, salmon, bears, beavers, deer, wolves, eagles, and ravens often used their magical qualities to bring about spectacular events. They could also become part of a family social unit and be incorporated into the crests of that group.

Nochnochs were also real entities with tremendous powers. Boas calls them nExnô'x, helpers from Heaven, and points out that the term designates anything mysterious.[6] As well as being supernatural helpers, they are also the whistles used in dances and the sleight-of-hand tricks of the dancer. Ken Harris says that they are either persons or animals possessed by known spirits and used by the Heavenly Father to punish or reward. The nochnoch, therefore, wields a large influence in the Northwest Coast peoples' lives. Any action of a nochnoch is interpreted as either a punishment or a reward. Most of the myths are concerned with both good and evil. It is important in the stories that the moralizing force of goodness prevail.

Other versions of these myths have been published. Writers, scholars, historians, and Northwest Coast ethnographers have written various accounts of the myths belonging to the Indians. There are also hundreds of popular versions. None has hitherto appeared translated wholly by an Indian and from the Indian point of view. Marius Barbeau, in his The Downfall of Temlaham, which deals with many myths of the area called Damelahamid in this book, admits that his narrative "is couched in the author's own style and composition."[7] Boas remarks that he made the translation of his collection of tales, basing it on a free interlinear rendering by his informant.[8]

The present collection of myths is the work of Kenneth B. Harris, Hagbegwatku, who persuaded his uncle, Arthur McDames, to record them in 1948. They have not been tampered with in any way and are given exactly as translated by Ken Harris, using his own divisions and order. These are his stories, presented exactly as he understands them. He admits that there may be a few errors in the translation because there is a very fine

---

[6] Boas, Tsimshian Mythology, p. 543.

[7] Barbeau, The Downfall of Temlaham (Toronto: Macmillan, 1928), p. vii.

[8] Boas, Tsimshian Mythology, p. 31.

line separating past, present, and future tenses. Indian languages do not use tenses in the same way as do Indo-European languages. Also there are Indian words for which there is no English equivalent. These words have been left in the myths in Indian form. The spelling of the Indian words and names is his. It does not accord with the International Phonetic Alphabet, but approximates his own oral language in written English. Further cross-examination of the spelling on my part might well have interfered with the flow of translation, and this of course would have defeated the purpose behind the solely Indian recording of these particular myths. Ken Harris's comments relating to the individual tales appear before each story. A comparison with myths collected by Boas, Swanton, and Robinson, written by myself, has also been included.

These myths were originally taped in *Tsomalia*, described by Ken Harris as the mother tongue of the Gitksan and used by Arthur McDames. Ken's mother, Mrs. Irene Harris, a woman in her eighties, was one of the few people left who could translate them. Mrs. Harris agreed to translate the stories into his language for Ken who could then put them into English to be written down.

Oral tradition was broken. However, as far as possible, uncontaminated myths were now a written fact. The act of transposing oral tradition into written form was upsetting to Ken. It was an irrevocable changing of the old order. Also, he had to become familiar with a tape recorder and tell his myths without the benefit of a live and responsive audience. In oral tradition, the story teller would always stop and reflect at the most crucial part of the story and remind the listener of permanent instructions. He could then see or sense the response of the audience to his admonitions. For example, as Ken Harris says, "One of the first instructions emanating from the nature of our people, originating with our Heavenly Father, is that you have to be conscious of certain things. You have to be able to differentiate between right and wrong. What is good does not harm the people. What is wrong leads to sheer destruction. This is a way of saying 'The moral of the story is . . . .' " This kind of reflection or exhortation is omitted in the printed version.

Myths demand time, both to tell and to be absorbed. These should not be read quickly. They have been preserved for centuries, retold countless times with deep feeling and concern, and should be read with respect and reflection.

Mrs. Irene Harris had a remarkable life. She was old enough to have heard these myths first before the turn of the century. She had seen and lived through many changes in the Indian way of life. Ken's father was her third husband. About five feet in height, she had a dignity of bearing usually associated with a much taller person. All her life she had known herself to be a princess and the top-ranking woman of a matrilineal society. For me she was at least three separate people. A member of the Salvation Army, wearing the uniform of General, she became the embodiment of that religion. In western clothes, she was a charming, witty, and sprightly *raconteur*. In full Indian regalia she was undoubtedly the matriarch, almost unapproachable.

One of the many stories she shared with me referred to the coronation of Queen Elizabeth to which she had been personally invited and a seat had been saved for her in Westminster Abbey. On the eve of her departure she said, "I was poisoned, dear, poisoned by my own people, who did not want me to go, to leave the country. I was so sick, I couldn't go." She added, "I don't blame them. I am not angry. I understand."

Mrs. Harris did meet the Queen. On her 1970 visit to British Columbia for the centennial celebrations, Queen Elizabeth and Irene Harris met and chatted in Prince Rupert. The Queen was intrigued with Mrs. Harris's regalia and asked her about the historical abalone- and ermine-trimmed headdress she was wearing. It seems a fitting curtain-call to a long, eventful life. Shortly afterwards, Mrs. Harris suffered a stroke and remained speechless for her remaining few months.

Ken Harris has inherited his mother's bearing and dignity. To a greater extent than most people are capable of, he has successfully managed to live in two worlds, that of his Indian ancestors and the twentieth-century life of Prince Rupert. He speaks of his decision to embrace both worlds. "Some years ago, after the order of our system, I had a choice of marrying Indian princesses from different clans who were picked for myself. At that time I was very much oriented towards our new civilization and I wasn't prepared to follow the order of our people. So I left. I went away. I joined the Services and I went to the Royal Officer's School, R.C.A.F., at London, Ontario. I stayed with the R.C.A.F. for the duration of my training as an Officer Cadet and then I got my release. During this time, I met a very beautiful girl from the Prairies, an Indian girl. She was a princess. I courted her and I married her. She immediately won the hearts of our people, particularly the Raven Clan." His wife was adopted into the clan and into the chief's house and given a Northwest Coast Indian name.

The title of this book, *Visitors Who Never Left*, comes from two sources. You will learn the identity of one visitor who arrived "over thousands of years ago" and who is still attending today's ceremonies. This link has remained unbroken with the contemporary "visitor" appointed from the ranks of the living, in accordance with age-old tradition. For the rigid seating-plan of a feast, *Hagbegwatku*, " first born," still sits at the right hand of the "visitor" who was so long ago granted the central place of honour. The other "visitors" in the title who remained are the people of *Damelahamid* themselves, who came to earth from Heaven, bringing the Indian people their culture, and staying in their earthly paradise.

Ken Harris believes that all the Indians of the Northwest Coast who practise the clan system and erect totem poles were one people originally. Though linguists would not agree, he bases his premise on the Indian word for the Skeena River — *Kshian*. *Damelahamid* was on the banks of the *Kshian* and the first people who lived there were called *Gitshian*. *Git* means "people," and *Gitshian* means "people of the *Kshian*." As some moved towards the mouth of the Skeena, they became known as the *Tsimshian* or "people who live in the basin of the *Kshian*." Southward, on the coast, are the *Salikshian*, or Salish people as they are known today. *Salikshian* means "people *from* the *Kshian*." Further away live the *Wakakshian* or "people who originated *in* but now live all the way *from* the *Kshian*."

Using such folk-etymology, Ken Harris also believes that the *Kwakiutl* or "potlatch people" as he calls them, get their name from the *Tsomalia* word *Kwakiugit* and, as they practise the same clan system, have totem poles, and share the same type of feasts, they also descend from *Damelahamid*. The Queen Charlotte Islands were known as *La Haidah*: *Haidah* in *Tsomalia* means "it seemingly comes out of the horizon and stands up straight from the horizon." The first people from *Damelahamid* who saw these islands so spoke of them, and the Indians who settled on them became known as *Githaidah*. In Alaska, the Tlingits were originally called *Katlingiut* in *Tsomalia*. They are believed to be warriors from *Damelahamid* who moved into the north and never returned.

There is one difficulty with fitting the remaining people — the *Nishga* of the upper Nass — into this pattern. Ken Harris maintains that they were people who never moved very far from *Damelahamid*. He says that some of his people believe that the *Nishga* may have migrated into their present area from the north and become known first as *Tiglutshian* or "people of the Ice." Whichever, is right, the *Nishga* now practise the old culture. These theories proposed by Ken Harris provide an interesting follow-up to the migrations of the people of *Damelahamid* as described in the myths.

These myths, then, belong to the Indians. Through the efforts of Mrs. Irene Harris and Kenneth B. Harris, and with the generous support of the Canada Council, this book was possible. There are many other people who have contributed. The late Professor Ian McNairn of the Department of Fine Arts and Professor Wilson Duff of the Department of Anthropology, both at the University of British Columbia, supported the project from the onset. Michael Robinson, a student of anthropology, introduced me to myth analysis. Jane Fredeman, Editor of the University of British Columbia Press, gave patient and valuable assistance. June Binkert spent hours typing the manuscript. I owe special thanks, also, to my husband who introduced me to Ken Harris and then followed the progress of the project with interest and insight. The culmination of this effort is dedicated to Mrs. Irene Harris who died before she could see the result of her labour. I feel she, somehow, knows how it turned out.

Frances M. P. Robinson
Vancouver, August 1974.

Foreword

This is Ken Harris speaking. I will attempt to translate the history of our people of *Damelahamid* as it was told by Arthur McDames who was the Chief of *Damelahamid* and my mother, Mrs. Irene Harris, who explained the meaning of the Indian terms to me. I also speak for myself as I am the last source of such information and as I hold the title of *Hagbegwatku*, First Born of our Nation. I feel that this information must be passed on to my relatives and clansmen. Because of the changing times and the fact that our people are now in a transition period, my choice of media, the printed word, is essential. There is no longer the time to tell the myths as we used to in the old days.

Many non-Indian friends have made kind words of encouragement and I would like to express my sincere appreciation to all.

I extend very special thanks to Frances Robinson who occupies a very special place in my heart, in the hearts of my family, and in the hearts of the people of *Damelahamid*, for her great help in the publication of this work. In recognition of this valuable assistance I, *Hagbegwatku* of *Damelahamid*, confer the title of *Bigetdeda* (a princely title meaning "occupying the key position") on her at this time. This, in effect, means that I have adopted her as my sister.

Dem gam ae yeas Bigetdeda.

PLATE 2.   (*above*) Mount Rocher Deboule or *Stekyawden*, overlooking Hazelton

PLATE 3.   (*left*) Poles at Skeena Crossing; one-horned goat seen on the left

PLATE 4.   (*overleaf*) Poles at Kitwanga

PLATE 1.   Skeena River, "River of Mists"

Photographs by Frances M. P. Robinson

PLATE 5. (*left*) Ermine and abalone ceremonial hat, the *lan num ghide*

PLATE 6. (*right*) *Medeek* blanket showing the slaying of the *Medeek* by *Tso ech* and *Yabadets*

PLATE 7. (*below*) Seeley Lake, *Mean tse kho don*, home of the *Medeek*

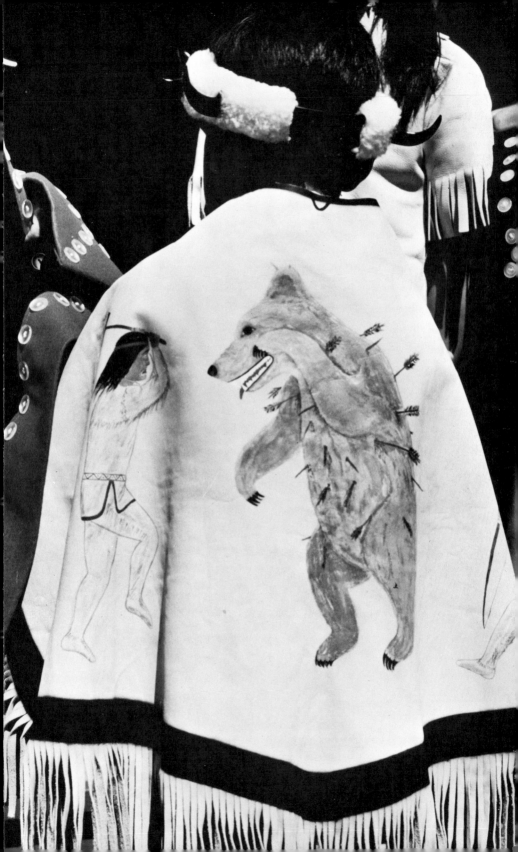

PLATE 8. Detail of pole at Kitsegucla   PLATE 9. Killer Whale pole at 'Ksan

IN THE BEGINNING

Story One tells of the origin of the people of *Damelahamid*, emphasizing the supernatural element. The people of *Damelahamid* were not the first people on earth, but they were the first to introduce a culture to the Northwest Coast area stressing the relationship of the people with their Father-in-Heaven and starting a matrilineal system.

1.

The Two Villages

Ken Harris points out that in the olden days people were not buried but were cremated or "burned." He adds, "Even today when we invite people to our burial ceremonies, we ask them to come to our burning ceremony."

Another interesting point is that the difference between calling a settlement a village, a town, or a city is merely a matter of emphasis in the myth itself. It can also refer to the actual site. A small village, if important according to the rank of the people living in it, would be emphasized and emerge as a city in the telling. *Damelahamid*'s size is illustrated by two sayings: "It is so large you don't know your neighbours," and, "When a flock of geese flies over *Damelahamid*, people go out in the street and shout and make other noises to confuse the birds, and the birds, exhausted, fall to the ground before they are able to traverse the whole city."

It is told that before the known civilization of the Northwest Coast Indians, there lived on the banks of *Tselisam* a large number of people. There were two villages, one born on each side of the river. The exact location of the villages is not known. Each village had a chief, but there is no reference made to any evidence that the civilization is after the pattern of our known civilization. Nor is there any memory telling the names of the chiefs or their relationship to one another.

There lived in one of these villages the chief and his seven sons. It was about the time of the Beaver Hunt. The seven sons prepared themselves for this event. Part of the preparation procedure was a strict code of ethics. A married couple had to observe the purity of their relationship that was consummated in the company of the pledge of unity. To even consider a

3

relationship with a stranger at this time was a bad omen and brought foul luck to the hunting party. Other forms of preparation were the eating of Devil's Club. The bark was peeled off and the fat that was exposed was chewed and the juice was swallowed. Bathing in a running creek four nights in a row was another proper method of preparation.

The seven brothers set out for the beaver area. They went to a lake not too far removed from the villages. This lake was created by a large beaver dam. And beaver were plentiful. The brothers trapped, and six out of the seven were successful. They trapped for several days and it was always the same six brothers who caught beaver, while the oldest brother found that the beavers shunned his traps. The beaver even showed their contempt by springing his traps.

He became very sad, even though his brothers gave him one beaver apiece each time they visited their traps. He was not happy at all. He guessed by now that the strict observance of the code of ethics was being flaunted at home. He was very angry at the keen sense of the crafty beaver in knowing all these things.

When it came time to pack up their traps, he called his brothers and told them of his contempt for the beaver who had obviously taunted him purposely. He told them that when day came he would break the beaver dam in retaliation. His brothers tried to appease their elder brother by making more gifts of beaver pelts. But his mind was now made up and he was, after all, the eldest.

The next day he set out to execute his plans. He went to the centre of the huge beaver dam and found the key log that held the dam secure. It was his plan and it was he who would execute the destruction of the beaver dam. It was now early spring and the run-off had created a huge force behind the dam. In his grief and self-pity he was blind with hatred. He pulled the log and the force of dammed-up water broke the dam with such sudden force that he got washed down the stream with the debris.

They soon recovered their brother's body and found that the key log had gone right through his body. It had gone right through his heart. It was obviously the work of evil, so they made a plan. They planned to burn their brother, and they did.

They picked up all their belongings and headed back to their village. They called it *Weguljeb* and that means a city. They got back in the middle of the afternoon but they did not enter their home. They camped outside, and when it was dark they moved in very cautiously and came to their father's house where all their wives were living around the hut. Each section of the house was allocated to a different brother and his wife, or to his wife alone while they were on the trapline. They came in close. They visited each sleeping area of their wives and they found their wives were sound asleep. They could hear them snoring. They came to their oldest brother's wife's sleeping area and heard all kinds of laughter — gaiety — and goings on. They recognized their brother's wife's voice in her gaiety, and they also heard a strange man's voice with it.

They waited until the entertainment was over and obviously the two had gone to sleep. And they went into the house and they told their father, the chief of the house, what had happened. They told him that their oldest brother had met with an accident and that he was dead and that they had buried him.

They told him of their plan and he said nothing. He was very sad and he was ready for anything that his sons were prepared to do. But their mother who had heard the story also and who heard of their plan attempted to warn her oldest daughter-in-law and made a loud noise lamenting, and the chief of the house scolded her.

"Why are you lamenting in such a form in the middle of the night?" And she told him, "I had a dream. I had a very bad dream that my son had met with an accident and he was dead. I had a very bad dream that my oldest son was dead." But the rest of the house had no idea what she was talking about. They didn't take the warning.

So, later on, when everybody was asleep, the brothers entered again and they took a skinning knife called a *ha goelhz* which they always used and they cut the visitor's head off. They took the head with them and they tied the long hair in a knot and put a pole through it and stuck it up in the gable of the house. It was hung over the entrance of the door. During this time the body which was headless was still very active or still alive, and it rolled over on a baby which was right next to it and the baby started to cry. The chief and his wife knew by this time what had happened and so they asked their son's wife, "What is going on? Why aren't you attending to that baby?" And she said, "It will take a little while. The baby has made a mess and I am working on it." What she was actually doing was digging a hole in the ground next to her sleeping quarters. She dug a hole and buried the rest of the body and everything was quiet. They all went back to sleep.

The young man who had come to visit her came from the other village on the opposite side of the river. He had brought a servant with him, a servant who travelled with him everywhere he went, and this servant was in the canoe by the river's side waiting for his master to return. This hadn't happened for a long time and he knew where to look for his master when he hadn't shown up. So a smart little servant he was.

He decided to take chunks of wood and went to the house where his master was. He knocked at the door and they let him in and they asked him, "What are you here for?" They suspected that he must be missing his master. He said, "I've come to get some fire from your fire because our fire is out on the other side of the river."

And they said, "How come you came so far to get your fire?"

And he said, "I would have gone to the other houses, but their fires are all out, too."

So they told him, "Go ahead. Help yourself with the fire."

So he stuck the wood into the fire and waited for it to burn properly and he picked it up. He looked around the house. He observed everything very earnestly and he couldn't find his master. As he stepped through the door after he had taken his fire, a chunk of blood fell from the gable and landed right on his bare feet. He looked down at his bare feet and saw that it was a great big chunk of fleshy blood that had fallen on his toes and he looked up to see where it had come from.

Lo, to his surprise, he stared right at the face of his master hanging from the gable, bodiless. He immediately threw the fire away and after the order or the fashion that is normally told about servants, he threw himself on to the ground and rolled in the dirt. He rolled in the dirt, mourning, showing his loyalty to his master. He mourned and he rolled all the way down to his canoe.

He got into his canoe and he went across the river. He ran up to his master's house and told the chief, who was his master's father, what had happened. The chief immediately called his people together and he said, "We will have to avenge the death of my son. Be prepared for battle." And they were prepared for battle.

In the meantime, the village on the other side of the river was prepared for battle and the people were ready. The warriors came. They came in hordes by canoes and the battle began. The village that was under attack was gaining. They were gaining admirably. They were obviously the superior side in battle.

Angry, one of the brothers thought that if it hadn't been for the woman there would have been no battle at all. If she hadn't been so foolish as to betray her husband, there would have been no battle at all. So he took a large tree and sharpened it. He chopped it off at the top and sharpened it, and he took the girl and mounted her on the tree. The tree entered from the end and went through her body. This happened on the top of a hill.

The girl's immediate relatives saw this and they were very sad. They were very angry now at the brothers. They were not concerned about the village any more. They turned on the brothers. They turned on the brothers and their family and

7

suddenly the attacking village found allies in some of the other villagers. Pretty soon the village under attack was wiped out. It was wiped out completely and this meant that only a few survived. The attacking villagers did not consider the fact that some of the enemy were aiding them and they had slain them all, also.

Analogues

The Swanton collection of *Haida Texts and Myths* contains two versions of these early village peoples: the "Story of the Two Towns that stood on Opposite Sides of Nass River" as told by Jimmy Sterling of the StA'stas People,[1] and the second part of "A-Slender-One-Who-was-Given-Away" related by John Sky of Those-born-at-Skedans.[2] In the first story a menstruant woman and her mother were saved; otherwise the tale develops along similar lines to that told by Ken Harris. In the second story, the two villages are identified as Q!ado' and Metlakahtla, a daughter and her mother survive, and the beaver hunt occupies a smaller portion of the whole tale. Stories of two rival towns were popular among both the Tsimshian and the Haida.

---

[1] John R. Swanton, *Haida Texts and Myths* (Washington, D.C.: Government Printing Office, 1905), p. 341.

[2] Ibid., p. 159.

2.

The Two Survivors and the Search for a Husband

The cry of the grandmother, *"Nalhzdum an nex cu tloeh goe/Dem an ská-twa-m,"* does two things. It invites something of a supernatural order to happen. This explains why all the animals were capable of replying. And it explains the origin of the grandmother's name. *Ská twa* became a title. There is no one bearing it now.

The grandmother lived an earthly existence and therefore she could not be transported into the supernatural world. Her grand-daughter, however, was still pure and could make the journey.

There was only one elderly woman who was looking after her grand-daughter left. In those days when a woman started to menstruate for the first time she was put into a special surroundings. She was not allowed to mix with society. She was kept in this special house until after she had completed her period. Only one attendant was allowed to visit her and this was the order. It was her grandmother who was with this girl. She took the girl and ran away with her up the mountainside away from all the battle. They were the only two who were saved from the battle.

They sat down. They could see the village from where they sat and they saw that everybody was finished. It was all over. And the grandmother was very sad. Then she remembered out of pity for herself and her grand-daughter that they needed a man to fortify their family and a strange thing happened. The grandmother started to shout to the four winds of the earth. She shouted these words, asking for or inviting a husband for her grand-daughter. She said:

Nalhzdum an nex cu tloeh goe
Dem an skā-twa-m.

Several forms of life answered her call. All who answered the call were in the form of a man. A squirrel answered her call in the form of a man. A man would suddenly appear and say, "I will marry your daughter." The grandmother would then ask this question, "If we are under attack, how would you protect us?"

And the man would immediately perform his capability for protection. The squirrel, for instance, would run up and down the tree, grind his teeth and make all kinds of noises.

Everything came. Rabbits. All forms of animal came to answer her call.

A grizzly bear came and she just about gave in. The grandmother was afraid when the grizzly bear started to growl. But then she remembered that man kills grizzly bears and there were a lot of brave warriors who wouldn't stop at the growl of a grizzly bear. So she told him, also, "Go. You are not fit to protect me and my grand-daughter."

Everything had answered her call. All earthly forms of life had answered. The grandmother sat there and she was very sad. She was very sad because she knew that no one else would answer. But she tried again and she shouted:

Nalhzdum an nex cu tloeh goe
Dem an skā-twa-m.

Suddenly a fog came in low and it settled right around them. And out of this fog stood a very brilliant looking young man and he answered in a different form. Previously, when any of the forms of life had answered her, they said, "I will marry your daughter." But this man had a different tone. "My dear lady, don't you think that maybe I can probably marry your daughter?"

The grandmother looked at him and found that his form of life was very different. It was unusual. It was just like light. And the grandmother asked, "What are you going to do to protect us when we are being attacked?"

10

The young man took what is known as a *tja-hō* made from wood and very small. He took the *tja-hō* and pointed it to the east and started to move it to the west and the earth started to tilt. It started to tilt and *Skā twa* and her grand-daughter hung on for their dear lives and immediately the grandmother said, "Hold it! Hold it! Hold it! Let me think this over."

So she thought for a while and then she said, "Well, this could be true." She asked the young man again, "How are you going to protect us?" And he did the same thing. This time *Skā twa* was convinced and she didn't even consider it again. She said, "All right. All right. You are going to be my new son-in-law. I know now that you have powers that nobody else on earth has."

He stopped at that and he said, "All right. We are going on a journey. We are going on a long trip. I am going to have to take you through space, but I do not want you to open your eyes. It doesn't matter what you hear or what happens, because if you open your eyes and try to see what happens, it will be perilous for all of us."

So he took the young lady under his right arm. Up to this time there was no known name for her. Because of the nature of the way her grandmother called for and made a husband for her, the grandmother was given the name *Skā twa* from her cry. She said:

Nalhzdum an nex cu tloeh goe
Dem an skā-twa-m.

and her name was born then: *Skā twa*.

So the young man took *Skā twa* also, and put her under his left arm and they closed their eyes and they all flew. *Skā twa* heard a lot of noises that frightened her, so she opened her eyes and fell back to earth. They all fell flat on earth and the young man said, "Obviously you are not prepared to go where I am taking you." He took a branch from one of the old spruce trees nearby, pulled it out, and took his mother-in-law and pushed her into the hole and covered it up again. And he said, "To the end of time people will hear you." To this day, when the

11

wind blows, you hear a howling in the spruce trees. The old Indians used to say that it was *Skā twa*. "She is still reminding us of how our beginning started."

Then the man took the young lady and they flew and finally they landed. She did not open her eyes. She heard several things that frightened her but she did not open her eyes. Finally they landed and the young man said, "All right, you can open your eyes now." And they were in a strange place, a beautiful and a strange place.

Analogues

The Jimmy Sterling version collected by Swanton lists the contenders for the young girl's hand in marriage as Grouse, Sparrow, Blackbird, Other Birds, Deer, Black Bear, Grizzly Bear, Beaver and all Forest Animals, with, finally, the "son of Supernatural-being-of-the-shining heavens" arriving and being accepted.[1] In the John Sky version, the order is Grizzly Bear, Beaver, and Deer, before a strange being "carrying a bow with feathers on it for a staff and holding arrows in his hand appeared. He wore dancing leggings and a gable-crowned hat. When he took a heavy step with his right foot the earth cracked." He is described as the son of "One-who-goes-along-above (i.e., the moon)."[2]

[1] Swanton, *Haida Texts*, p. 342.
[2] Ibid., p. 167.

3.

The Happenings in Heaven

Ken Harris says that Indians have always emphasized virgin births. The bath mentioned in the corner of the house was a kind of waterfall that came out of the corner of the house and disappeared into the ground.

The names *Liggeyoan, Akagee* and *Goestella* are still in use today for princes and princesses. The box, the *hawlhz-ganku*, is recognized as being an important gift from the Father-in-Heaven. This Indian word is only used on two other occasions when a particular box is mentioned in connection with a supernatural being. The significant pole, the *gilhast*, gets its name from *gil* meaning *only* or *prime* and *hast* meaning *pole*.

The Father-in-Heaven is recognized as the Creator. His Indian name is *Simoigetdamla ha.* He is also referred to as the Heavenly Father. *Simoiget* means First Man or chief. When the white man appeared with his Christian God, the Indians were satisfied that He was the same as their own.

They were in a strange place, a beautiful and a strange place and they were obviously in front of the chief's house because it was so different. Everything about it was different. And the young man said, "Come, enter with me and you will meet my family." And she did.

The chief of the house, the young man's father, said, "There is a bath in the corner of the house. You will bathe this young lady."

They put her under it. The servants took all her clothes off and they put her under the water. And the waters just peeled her skin. Her appearance was different. She was very much like the people who had taken her. They were all different. They were just like light. She became different and the chief of the house directed her to her quarters called *tyak tyak*.

13

She went and they gave her a mat to sleep on. She laid on it. And her husband-to-be, he who accepted her for his wife, went upstairs to a higher balcony where he lived. The sun seemed to appear from where he was and shone upon her. He never saw her again. Only the beam of the sun, as she interpreted it, was shining upon her.

In short order she became pregnant. And she had a boy — a baby boy — and his grandfather took the boy. He took him into the corner and washed him. He washed him, washed him well, and then he stretched him. The boy grew by feet. In short order she got pregnant again. And she had another boy. The same thing happened. The grandfather took the boy and washed him in the bath in the corner and then stretched him. Not too long after, she was pregnant again and a girl this time was born. The grandfather did the same thing. He took her to the corner and washed her and stretched her.

Now all this was a very unusual thing. This young lady had not known men. She had menstruated for the first time and after the order of our time a girl did not marry until after she menstruated and she does not know men. The young lady had not known anybody and these were very unusual births for her to have children and still not know a man.

But the grandfather was ready now. He had given them names. They were quite grown-up now and they had names. The first one was called *Liggeyoan*. The second born was *Akagee* and the little girl was given the name *Goestella*. Now these names were designed for different purposes. *Liggeyoan* was to be the elder and the leader of the three, and *Akagee*, his brother, and their sister, *Goestella*, were all to return to earth.

The grandfather made preparations to send them back to earth. He gave them instructions. He told them, "There are several things that you have to do. One of them is to avenge your people and I will give you what you need to do this." He pulled out a box, a decorated box, and in this box, the *hawlhzganku*, there was a pole — a very small pole. It had absolutely

14

nothing on it. It was straight and true. And in this box there was a hat, a hat known as *lan num ghide*. It had ermine fur on it and also very brilliant stones. He also gave them the *tja-hō*, the name given to the instrument that was used when their mother was first picked up, and this instrument was to be the tool of destruction for the time when they were to avenge their relatives on earth.

The grandfather told them several things that were going to happen. He said, "When you go back to earth, you are going to avenge your people."

He also gave them a little box known as *goldum tsean*. This was a gambling box and it was a common thing in those days to use this type of gambling box. There were two little sticks. One was marked and the other one wasn't. The chips that they used then were these marked sticks. These sticks represent different things or different values. And so he gave them these things and he told them, "When you get back to earth, you are going to challenge the chief of the other village. I will give you all this material that you are going to lose. You are going to lose, and when you lose too much you are going to become very angry and you are going to have to kill the chief. This will be the beginning of your revenge."

And he says, "After this is all done I am going to remove you from this area and I am going to place you in a new land. This new and beautiful land you are going to call *Damelahamid*. At this new place you are going to build your new house, your new home. And in front of your new home I want you to plant this little pole that I have given you. And this little pole, you will find, will grow all by itself. It is going to grow to pierce the sky and the name will become known as *gilhast*. You are going to build your home according to these specifications. You are going to have twelve logs in the front, twelve logs at the back, and twelve logs on the sides, and these homes you are going to build from one generation to the other. Because there will come a time when there will be a flood. It is going to be a big flood. And when this time comes a lot of people will run away from this flood. They will go to the highest mountains. But you won't. You and your family will stay in your home, your *dakh*. And you are going to cut this great big pole down, the *gilhast*, and are going to use it as braces. You are going to brace or reinforce your *dakh*. This is what you are going to call your new home — a *dakh*.

"You are going to brace your *dakh* with the *gilhast* and you are not going to run away. You are going to survive the flood because you are chosen to survive this flood."

When all the instructions were finished, the grandfather took them and placed them in a little canoe along with the box that he had given them.

The grandfather gave them the *hawlhz-ganku* in which were the *lan num ghide*, which was to be the crown of *Damelahamid*, and the tree that was going to grow itself and which became known as the *gilhast*, and the *tja-hō*. The *tja-hō* began, too, as a special instrument. There was only one known in the world and it was used for one purpose only. So the grandfather put them in a canoe and he placed them on earth.

Analogues

The Jimmy Sterling version mentions five boys and one girl being born of the marriage of the young woman and son of Supernatural-being-of-the-shining heavens, with the grandfather's present being the innermost box of a nest of five, plus a small wedge, a knife, and medicine.[1] The John Sky version tells of the wife of One-who-goes-along-above giving birth to eight boys and two girls, with both females having the power of healing. The grandfather's box appears later in the story.[2]

[1] Swanton, *Haida Texts*, p. 343.
[2] Ibid., p. 168.

Boas records an incident of a father washing a young son and then pulling him in order to make him grow quickly.[3] Swanton tells of a father who put his feet on his son's feet, and by pulling, made him grow up.[4]

---

[3] Boas, *Tsimshian Mythology*, p. 839.
[4] Swanton, *Haida Texts*, p. 338.

4.

The Gambling Game

The name *Tsim ham haemid* is the Earth Name for the Heavenly-born *Goestella* who was given powers of miraculous healing.

All of a sudden in the area where the two villages were on opposite sides of the river a very thick fog came in. The canoe landed on their own side of the river. The fog lifted on their side but it remained on the other. When they got out of their canoe, they found that there were some copper shields lying around. So they started to gather all the copper shields and they started to build a house made out of copper. They made noises while they were constructing this building. They made the sounds of metal clanging together. Bing! Bing! Bing! The people on the other side of the river, still in the fog, heard these noises and the young people — the foolish people — started to shout, "Oh, if the people of that village who are trout-eaters would have not been so foolish, their voices from the dead would not have been heard."

The warriors of the village immediately got together. They were going to cross the river and dispose of any survivors who might have come back to the old village. But the elders, the wise people, told them, "Leave them alone. It is well that maybe one or two have survived the slaughter."

So they did. And, finally, later in the day, the fog lifted and they saw some people on the other side of the river. Three of them. Two of the people, both young men, got into a canoe and came across. They landed on the shore and pulled up their canoe. Several people came to meet them, and said, "What do you people want?"

The two young men told them, "Take us to your chief. We want to gamble with him. We have brought our own gambling box and we brought all the material to gamble with."

They took the two young men to the chief and the chief looked at them and said, "Well, my dear people, come on in. What do you want?"

And they said, "We have come to gamble. We have come to gamble with you." They put out their material and they sat down in the form and the passion of gambling. They took out the little *tja-hō* and laid it on the mat in front of them. They started to lose as they had been instructed to do. They lost and they lost. Finally, the chief kept looking at the little *tja-hō*, which was very small, and he said, "What are you people going to do with this little thing?"

And they said, "It is a *tja-hō*," and they just laughed at him.

Later on, they kept losing, and the chief said again, "Just what do you think you can kill with this little thing?"

They were getting ready for the end, and the elder one said, "It is wise not to ask. You might find out." And they went on. Finally they took all of their gambling equipment. They put it back in their box very quickly and the senior of the two picked up the little *tja-hō*, walked up to the chief very politely and banged him on the head with it very lightly. He fell forward on the mat, dead.

Before the people of that house realized what had happened, they had slipped out of the house and into their canoe. The people tried to grab them and hold them, but couldn't. They were, after all, protected by the Spirit.

They soon found themselves on their own side of the river. By this time the village they had left was prepared. They were prepared in hordes again. They were going to go across the river and destroy the two young men with ease, and they were going to do it in numbers.

19

So they went across the river in numbers and the battle began. The two young men killed them like flies. Every time one of the marksmen from the other side of the river found his mark on one of the boys, *Tsim ham haemid*, who was given the power of healing, would come up very swiftly and remove the arrow and heal the wound by rubbing her hand over it.

The battle went on. When the boys were surrounded and becoming overcome by the hordes of people, fog would settle in very heavily and very quickly, and the people would find that they were killing each other. Then the fog would disappear and the people would re-appear again and the battle went on. It went on until every warrior from the other village was destroyed. Finally, the young men decided that this was the end.

So they took the *tja-hō*, and in the fashion that was once shown by their father, they pointed it to the east and they moved it to the west and, as the *tja-hō* moved, the earth where the village across the river stood turned and all the canoes turned with it. All the people were turned under the earth and only poplar twigs were left where the city had stood.

This was the end of the battle and the three people lived on.

Analogues

In the Jimmy Sterling version the five boys gambled with the occupants of the rival town. They took the cover off their grandfather's box and burned the other town. Four of the brothers were eventually killed by the people of the Stikine, but their sister survived and with her youngest brother travelled far inland. The boys' adventures afterwards differ considerably from the Ken Harris version.[1] In John Sky's version, the children were

[1] Swanton, *Haida Texts*, p. 344.

returned to earth across the water from Metlakahtla. After a fight between the two villages, the grandfather, on being appealed to for help, took a small square box and "opened five boxes, one within the other. He took from the last something (shaped like skeins of yarn), covered with the sky and tied up with rope. After he had looked down for a while, he threw it down upon the people of Metlakahtla. Then their legs only were visible." All of the people were then killed. These "Clouds-of-the-Killer" resemble the fog in the Ken Harris story. Metlakahtla was also burned, and the brothers and sisters journeyed down the Nass to a town at its mouth. Here they warred successfully against the Tlingits but were finally killed by the people of Stikine. One sister revived the youngest brother who goes inland, marries, and turns into a loon when he needs hair seals and halibut. Many adventures follow, all involved with avoiding shame wherever possible.[2]

[2] Ibid., p. 171.

5.

The Birth of Damelahamid

Ken Harris was interested in Walter Wright's version mentioned below. He said that as part of the Indian way of getting to understand relatives in different areas and of making sure that the myths remain faithful to the original, he lived with Walter Wright for three years from 1936-1939 and that Mr. Wright later lived with Ken's family for six months. They listened to each other's versions of the stories, and it became clear to Ken that Walter Wright's versions were Tsimshian in language and thought, not Gitksan.

The three young people decided that they must explore the rest of the river, so they headed downstream. They carried the *tja-hō*, the *lan num ghide* and the *gilhast* in their box, the *hawlhz-ganku*. Every time they came across some people they would destroy them and destroy them very swiftly using the *tja-hō* because this was especially designed for this purpose. Finally, they came to a river where they camped, and by this time they had made lots of enemies. When they camped they took the *tja-hō* and laid it on a rock next to their encampment so that it would be ready if they needed it. And they camped.

In the middle of the night word came to them that they must leave where they are now and go their chosen place, their promised land, *Damelahamid*. And they were transported in the middle of the night. They did not take the *tja-hō* with them because it was meant for them to forget it. The grandfather had decided that there was enough killing, enough vengeance, so he, in his wisdom, made them forget the *tja-hō*.

So they moved. They were transported in a mysterious way to their new townsite called *Damelahamid*, and they settled. And they built their house according to the specifications that were given to them. And they planted the *gilhast* in front of their house. Overnight, it grew and the next day they looked at it and it pierced the sky. This was the *gilhast* and the beginning of a new clan, the *Gisgahast*.

Analogues

Ken Harris's version appears to be the only one with the brothers and their sister travelling downstream until a message from their grandfather directs them to their promised land. They were then moved in a "mysterious way" to their new townsite called *Damelahamid*, and here they settled. They planted the *gilhast* and the new clan began.

Will Robinson in *Men of Medeek* relates Walter Wright's story of the "Guell Haast" in which the area of the Bear People is defined as south of Kitzeukla. Here a giant tree with a single Haast, or fireweed, growing out of the snow at its feet was discovered. The "Guell Haast," single fireweed, vanished, but from that day on it "has had its place on the totems to tell of the time of famine and how the salvation of the people was wrought."[1]

---

[1] Will Robinson (as told by Walter Wright), *Men of Medeek* (Kitimat: Northern Sentinal Press Ltd., 1962), p. 25.

PEOPLE OF *DAMELAHAMID*

This story is used as a lesson to demonstrate the law that one should not make fun of animals or abuse them. When this law is broken, punishment follows both swift and severe.

1.

The Fatal Game

Tsimdakh is the name given to the people who originated from the *dakhumhast*, the house of the eldest of the two brothers. His name prior to coming to *Damelahamid* was *Liggeyoan* and on earth was changed to *Hagbegwatku*, or "first born." Ken Harris says that he is now the *Hagbegwatku* of his people.

The "root cellar" referred to is, in Indian, an *anuwish-ū* It is a small cloistered place and could have been a hole dug in the ground or a cave in a hillside. *Anuwish-ū* means "buried room." The name is related to earth. The phrase "just become a lady" refers to a girl having her first menstrual period. Prior to that she was always referred to as a "girl." During her menstrual period she had to be kept separate from the rest of the people.

In the middle of the night *Liggeyoan*, *Akagee* and *Goestella*, their sister, were transported. They were transported from *Tselisam* to a new site called *Damelahamid*. After they had arrived there, they remembered the instructions telling them how to construct their new home. So they went about it.

They got logs and cut them according to the specifications. They excavated a hole and lined it with twelve logs on each end and twelve on the sides, and this they called a *dakh*.

When their *dakh* was complete, they took up their *hawlhzganku*. In it they had the little pole that they were instructed to plant in front of their *dakh*. They were instructed to plant it not too close to the front, but far enough away and they would see what would happen. They did this. They planted it, and during the night it grew. It grew out of sight. It pierced the sky. They looked at it and they talked about it and they called it the *gilhast* to give a meaning to this pole. They called their house *dakhumhast*. They called in the people from their surroundings. They invited them to what they inaugurated — a feast, now called a *potlatch*. They multiplied. They multiplied in large numbers.

Every day the eldest brother got up; he would kill a snow-bird and tie it to his arrow. Early in the morning he would get up, and he would shoot this arrow over the top of his *dakh*, and he would make a wish. He wished that his people would multiply like the snow-birds and that they would be large in numbers. And the town grew very huge. It became very large.

The people became restless. They started to want to do something and they created a sport — a game — and it was football. They took a bear's stomach and they filled it and then they kicked it. They had sides and they kicked the bear's stomach from morning until night.

At this time it is told about a young girl who had just become a lady. She was kept apart from the rest of the people. She was kept in a kind of a "root cellar" and this "root cellar" was equipped with call-lines made of strips of hides. Each line indicated what type of food, water or whatever else the young lady might need. And this young lady was going through this period and she was in the "root cellar." She heard very strange noises, but she kept very quiet and very still. When the noises were all over, she decided to call her servants. She was getting thirsty, so she pulled the call-line for water. Nobody answered it. She pulled the call-line for food. Nobody answered it. She pulled the line for service. Nobody answered it.

She became alarmed, and she left her root cellar and found there was nobody left in the city. There wasn't a person — not a dog — not a cat — there was nothing left. Everybody had gone. She couldn't understand it. She went from one house to the other. She went to her brother's house. She started to lament, lament loudly, and she was very grieved. She was grieved very badly.

She wiped her nose and rubbed it on her stomach. She had nothing to do. It really didn't have any meaning for her. It was just something to do. She was grieved, grieved beyond compare because she had found out that she was all alone. The whole village had disappeared. The houses were still there but the people had disappeared.

She went to one of her brother's houses and she found that he had been making a handle for his *helhz le gyawku*. She found shavings of the *skan milkst*. She took the shavings and put them in the lining of her gown around her stomach.

She went to another brother's house and found that he had been making snowshoes and she found shavings from the *skan tsnaugh*. She took the shavings and put them in the lining of her gown again around her stomach.

She did all this because she was grieved. There was no real reason or rhyme for it.

She went about and found a little red stone, a little red stone in one of her uncle's houses. Just out of grief, she picked it up and put it in her gown. The little red stone was called *meshum la-up*.

She went about and came to another uncle's house and found that he had been working on snowshoes, also. And she found on the floor a stone, a stone used to sharpen cutting tools, called *hae gae hesku*. So she took this little stone and put it in the crease of her gown around her stomach.

She picked up some shavings from a feather used to decorate snowshoes' webbing called *loggum melhz tjalhz*. She took the *loggum melhz tjalhz* and she placed it in the crease of her gown.

She went to her grandmother's sleeping area and found that she was gone also. She was very grieved. All she found was a little skinning knife that her grandmother had used for years. It was called *ha goelhz* and it was used for skinning or dressing salmon. She took the *ha goelhz* and placed it in the crease of her gown. She was very grieved and she was lamenting all the while.

Finally, she decided to settle down in her father's house. She was alone now. She had nothing else to do. So she settled down.

Much to her surprise, she became pregnant. She became pregnant and in no time — less than the specified time as the story tells us — she had a son. And she was quite surprised. She couldn't understand this. But she remembered what she had done during the time of her grief, so she decided to call this boy *Noelhz* — which was the first thing she did when she cleaned her nose and wiped it on her stomach. And the boy became known as *Noelhz*.

So it went on. Time passed and she became pregnant again within short order. She bore a child and again it was a boy. She recalled how she had placed the *skan milkst* in the crease of her dress and she called the boy *Goodip skan milkst*.

In short order, she became pregnant again and she had another boy. And this time she called him *Goodip skan tsnaugh*. In short order she repeated the cycle. She became pregnant again and she had another boy. This time she called the boy *Goo meshum la-up*. Again she had another child and she recalled how she had put the stone used to sharpen cutting tools in her gown and she called the child *Goodip hae gae hesku*.

And she became pregnant again. She recalled how she had taken the shavings from the feather used to decorate snow-shoes' webbing. And she called the child *Goo loggum melhz tjalhz*. And she became pregnant again. It was a little girl and she was very happy. She remembered the skinning knife and she called the little girl *Goo ha goelhz* and this was complete.

All the things that she had picked up and put in her gown she had named her children. And she had one, two, three, four, five, six boys and one girl — the number of times that she had done these things. Seven children altogether.

Analogues

Walter McGregor of the Sealion-town people in "How a Red Feather Pulled up some People in the Town of Gunwa" combines the children playing their game of knocking a tree burl around and the subsequent floating feather with a young menstruant girl's strange pregnancies.[1] Ken Harris separates the game and the pregnancies into two stories and uses a bear's stomach for the football. In the McGregor version there are nine boys and one girl born in *Gunwa*, a Nass town. The feather eventually caused a heavy snowfall which caused the boys to travel and, after many adventures, only two survive by running safely under the edge of the sky. Swanton points out that this story is paralleled by a Masset myth, set in a Haida town.

In the Boas collection, the people in "The Story of Nalq" are all playing games in the night and the feather pulled everyone but a young princess into the sky.[2] Four boys and one girl were born from unusual pregnancies. Boas collected six versions — Tsimshian, Nass, and Haida — of this story, one mentioning *T!Em-lax-ā'm* on a large prairie, one from *Gunwa*, others from a beach town, all with either one female surviving, or with a grandmother and an adolescent girl, or a mother and her daughter. Boas also found an analogous Haida tale, a composite of the story of a jealous uncle who set adrift his nephew and the feather story. He also mentions a corresponding Tlingit tale located in Haida country.[3] He points out that a child originating from the tears and the mucus of the woman who has been spared is a world-wide theme.

---

[1] Swanton, *Haida Texts*, p. 330.
[2] Boas, *Tsimshian Mythology*, p. 125.
[3] Ibid., p. 734.

2.

The First Punishment of Damelahamid

This very important part teaches our people that they must not mock or make fun of animals.

They all lived on in *Damelahamid* and the seven children grew fast. They grew very fast, very rapidly. One day they found the ball that the people of *Damelahamid* had made for recreation.

They found the ball and they found it was very nice to kick, and they kicked it and they followed it around. They kicked it and then they started passing it to one another, kicking it to one another. They found out very rapidly how to use the ball. They were enjoying it, enjoying it very much.

Their mother saw all this and she got after them. She scolded them. She said, "You must not do this. I have no idea what happened to all our people, but I do know that they were playing. They were playing with that same ball you are playing with, and it is forbidden by our people to mock any part of the animal kingdom. We take what we have to eat and we do not waste. This is the law of our people. Our Father-in-Heaven does not allow us to waste or to mock. So I feel that the reason why they disappeared was because they were doing exactly what you are doing now — playing with that ball made from a bear's stomach."

But they didn't pay any attention to her. And one day, while they were playing, they observed that a white feather came floating down from the heavens. It floated down very gently and it stopped. They all stopped and watched it.

Noelhz, who was the most outspoken one of them and the one who was likely to do anything, ran for it and grabbed the little feather and stuck it on his head. He went back to kick the ball and he missed it. He looked down and found that he was suspended in air. So he shouted out to his brother, *Goodip skan milkst*. He said, "Oh, *Goodip skan milkst*, help me! I am in trouble!"

Goodip skan milkst came and grabbed him by the legs, and he grew roots and turned into a tree and went right to the bottom of the earth. There was a tug now — a tug from the feather — and soon *Goodip skan milkst* knew that his roots were going to give way. So he shouted, *"Goodip skan tsnaugh*, my brother, help me because I am in trouble!"

Goodip skan tsnaugh grabbed him by the legs and he became a tree and his roots went right into the ground. All of these children were returning to the same images that they had originated from. *Goodip skan tsnaugh* had now become a tree and his roots went right into the ground as he was holding down his brother. When his roots started to give way, he shouted, *"Goo meshum la-up*, help me! My roots are giving way!"

The little red stone helped him and a great big block of a boulder appeared. Soon this boulder started to lift and he shouted, *"Goodip hae gae hesku*, help me!"

Goodip hae gae hesku turned to stone and became a mountain, holding down the brothers who were being pulled into the heavens by the white feather. They started to lift again and they shouted to their brother, *"Goo loggum melhz tjalhz*, help!" So *Goo loggum melhz tjalhz* became a piece of feather that he used to be. But it did not help. They were still lifting. The feather was too light.

In the meantime, their sister, *Goo ha goelhz*, became very anxious. She was backwards and forwards and all of a sudden she started sharpening her hand and her hand became a skinning knife. And it became very sharp. She looked through it at the sun while she sharpened it, and she could see that it was becoming very sharp.

While they were still rising and being lifted up, she climbed up on top of them, jumping from head to head, right up to the feather. She took the feather and cut it right in half with her hand. The boys fell back to earth and they lay flat. This time they took their human forms again.

The little girl was not harmed. She was not hurt in the fall. Their mother came out and they were grieved. They were grieved. They were lamenting.

Goo ha goelhz, the little girl, said to her mother, "Let us put them in order and we will use this feather to revive them." So they did. She was obviously receiving instructions that she was not aware of.

They put the brothers in order and they covered them up with their blankets. And they walked around them with the feather — walked around them four times. At the end of the fourth time they all came back to life.

They realized now that they had done something wrong. They knew why the city of *Damelahamid* was punished. This was the first punishment of *Damelahamid* because they had defied the laws of nature, the laws of their god, the laws of their Father-in-Heaven who had instructed them not to torment animals, not to laugh at them, not to waste, and not to use any portion of the animal for amusement.

After *Goo ha goelhz* had revived her brothers, they went to their house and their mother told them of their history: how they came from Heaven and how their Heavenly Father left instructions and these instructions must not be broken under any circumstances. And they concluded that the same thing had happened to the rest of the city of *Damelahamid*, because that is what the other people had been doing. They had been playing ball. They had been playing football with a *tdek*, a ball made from the stomach of a bear.

So they lived on. That night when they went to sleep they

heard a windstorm and they heard a rattling, a great noise, that kept them awake most of the evening. It was a rattling of of what sounded like bones. And their mother said, "Don't anybody go outside. Don't anybody leave the house. You just stay in your beds."

And they did. In the morning they got up early and they went out. Lo and behold, they found scattered all over the countryside, among the houses in the village, bones — bones of dead people. They knew what had happened. So they gathered up the bones. They gathered them and their mother said, "Let us find the right bones for the right person, because they seem to have fallen in a pattern."

And they did. They put the bones together. And just out of their grief they covered a few bones that they had put together and they took the half-feather and walked around the bones. They walked around them four times and, lo and behold, they came back to life. And they found out it was their own people — people from their own house — their mothers and their fathers. They sat about putting the people together. They put bones together and laid them in order. There wasn't a person who was missing. Not a person. Not a dog. Not an animal was missing. They got them together. They put them together in order and they revived them with the half-feather.

There were times when they made a mistake. There were times when they took a shorter limb and placed it together or a longer limb and placed it together. When these people revived, they found one leg was too short or one arm was too short. These were the only obvious errors made. But the people were the same people they were before the heavens were angered and they were punished.

Analogues

In the second part, Ken Harris tells of a white feather (note that the feather is red in the Swanton collection) which carries off only the six boys. They are returned to life by their sister and their mother. The half-feather which the girl had obtained after using her sharp skinning-knife hand then revived the villagers who had died in the previous story following the first football game.

In both the Harris story and a Boas version the feather makes a few mistakes when reviving the village people.[1] Ken Harris mentions the wrong limbs being placed together and Boas adds wrong heads to wrong bodies — women's to men's — causing some women nowadays to have beards — or the wrong limbs to the wrong bodies, causing certain people to limp.

---

[1] Boas, *Tsimshian Mythology*, p. 736.

3.

Meeting the Spirits

This story tells how *Noelhz* makes the flat Prairie Provinces. It will be noted that the farther away from *Damelahamid* the stories occur, the more dramatic they become.

They all lived on and the brothers decided to explore. They decided to leave. They were going to explore the country because it was a big, beautiful country and they felt it must have something to offer. So the brothers left.

They took the feather with them. One of them put the feather in his headband and they left. They walked and they became very tired of climbing the mountains and going down into the deep of the valleys. They were getting very tired. So they took the feather and they stretched it across a ravine and the ravine immediately became flat. They had found a new method — a new way of travelling. They flattened the earth and they continued to travel. They did this; they flattened the earth, brought down mountains and filled out gulleys and filled up ravines.

On their journey they ran across a little old man. He was sitting by the river, sitting on a log beside the river. They passed by and then they stopped. *Noelhz*, the eldest, was also a very outspoken person. He stopped and talked to the old man. He said, "This is the wrong time of the year. Just what do you think you will catch in this river?"

The little old man with sarcasm said, "Oh, I was expecting

Noelhz to come up the river this way. That is why I am sitting here."

Noelhz was very angry but he didn't show it. He walked past the little old man and then he suddenly turned around and kicked him, kicked him into the water.

His brothers said, "What did you do that for? He seemed to be a gentle old man and he wasn't doing us any harm."

Noelhz said, "What's done is done." And they turned around and walked. They didn't go very far when they turned around to see where the little old man had been sitting. And there he was! He was sitting on the rock again!

Noelhz looked very angry. He rushed back and he kicked the little old man again and he seemed to fall into the water. But when *Noelhz* looked a little closer, he saw that the little old man hadn't fallen into the water. He had only flipped around to the other side of the rock and was hanging upside down. *Noelhz* was very annoyed at this. He was really annoyed. But he didn't do anything. He just walked away and they started to walk.

They came to an area they call *Spanachnoch*. This was an area where all kinds of monsters were found, a legendary area.

The brothers came into this area. They hadn't gone very far when they saw a house. They approached the house and they knocked at the door. The door opened. They saw a man sitting, sitting at the head of the house, and he had two heads.

The man said to the brothers, "Come in, my friends. I have been waiting for you. I knew you were coming this way, and I have been waiting for you."

The man got his servants to put down mats in honoured positions and the brothers sat there, waiting for something to eat.

Noelhz started to whisper to his brothers, "Heh, look at that man. How can a man be so ugly? He has got two heads. Are we going to sit here and eat his food?"

His brothers cautioned him and said, "Look, you are very outspoken and you have caused us nothing but trouble. Just keep your mouth shut." So *Noelhz* kept quiet for a while. Finally, he just couldn't resist. He had to speak a little louder. He wanted his host to hear him. He said to his brothers, "Heh, look at that man. Don't you think he is ugly? How can we stand to sit here and eat his food?"

The man got very angry. He took *Noelhz* and placed him between his two heads. *Noelhz* again returned to his original form before he was born. Some human waste from the nostrils was stuck like glue in between the two heads.

The two brothers, *Goo meshum la-up*, the red stone, and *Goodip hae gae hesku*, the sharpening stone, took their original forms as big boulders and plunged forward against the two-headed monster. They squashed him between them and they killed him. They took *Noelhz* and they walked around him with the feather and he became alive again. So they left. The two-headed man had once been a *nochnoch*.

They hadn't walked very far when they came across another house and they looked in. They saw a man sitting there. His hair was long. And bugs! Talk about bugs! Crawling up and down his hair! His hair was so full of bugs that *Noelhz* said, "Look at that monster! His hair is all full of bugs. This must be the grandfather of all bugs!"

The brothers said, "Look, we are getting very hungry and, after the order of hospitality, he is bound to feed us. So you just watch your mouth. Now be quiet and just let him be."

Before they had a chance to knock on the door, a voice came from inside. The man apparently knew that they were coming. After all, he was also a *nochnoch*. He called them in. He said, "Come on in, my friends. Be my guests." So they became guests of the house. They sat down and the servants started to prepare food. This time *Noelhz* was so hungry that he ate first. After they were full, he started to whisper again. He just couldn't keep it to himself. He said, "Isn't that man absolutely grotesque? Look at his hair! It's just full of bugs! I wonder if we ate some of them?"

His brothers gave him a good nudge in the ribs and told him,

"You just mind your mouth, *Noelhz*. He is a good man. He has obviously treated us gently and we are just going to leave him alone."

But *Noelhz* couldn't leave him alone. He wanted his host to know that he was very observant. So he said again, in a louder voice, loud enough for his host to hear it, "Look at that man! How can one man have so many bugs? He must be the grandfather of all bugs! I wonder if some of those bugs got into our food and we ate them?"

The man got angry and grabbed *Noelhz*. He just spread him all over his hair. *Noelhz* had turned into human waste from the nostrils again and he was spread all over the hair among the bugs and everything. He was doomed. But *Goo meshum la-up* and *Goodip hae gae hesku* again did their job and they soon squashed this *nochnoch*. They killed it. And they took *Noelhz* again and brought him back to life.

Analogues

The adventures of the six brothers carrying their feather that Ken Harris relates is paralleled by the adventures in Swanton.[1] In the latter, the feather caused a great snowfall, with the nine brothers seeking help. They killed a small animal but had later to revive it to appease its mother, an old woman. A "big thing" fell and squashed two of the boys, a small dog killed three, and the edge of the sky cut two in half. Only two survived.

Boas quotes many adventures for the brothers involving a blind cannibal, a raccoon and its grandmother Cliff House, a witch with sparks coming out of her mouth, and a cave which opens and closes killing two of them. In one version the plume melts an obstructing mountain. He discusses similar occurrences in the Tsimshian, Skidegate, and Nass River versions.[2]

---

[1] Swanton, *Haida Texts*, p. 331.
[2] Boas, *Tsimshian Mythology*, p. 738.

4.

The Journey Home

The hood is very important in this part. Young ladies in their first menstrual period had to wear a hood because they were not allowed to look at the sky. They were only allowed to look where they were going. The hood came right down over their heads and this prevented them from looking at people. The Indian word for the hood is *tgoi*. Because the person in this story was so huge she needed a large hood, and her name *Twe-tgoi-it* means "big hood."

The word "petrified" is used in a double sense. It means both severely frightened and also turned into stone.

They started to travel again. The brothers travelled and they had many adventures. And the same thing happened; every time they had to cross a ravine they would flatten it out with their feather. Finally, they decided they had to go home. They wanted to visit their own village and see their mother. So they started to return.

It was an easy journey going back. It was all flat land. But they were on their way back now. They were on their return trip. They came to a little river and they started to follow it. In their journey down this river on their way back to *Damelahamid*, they ran into a woman, a huge woman. She had a hood over her head. *Twe-tgoi-it* was the name given to this woman because of the nature of her hood.

The brothers were walking and they heard a noise. It went B-O-N-G! B-O-N-G! B-O-N-G! They stopped. They stopped dead in their tracks. They had heard of the *Twe-tgoi-it* who travelled. It was a *nochnoch*. They had heard how *Twe-tgoi-it* would transform people and make them petrified. So when they heard it, they said to one another, "Let us hide. Let us sit still here and hide. We don't want to disturb this person!" So they sat there.

Twe-tgoi-it was coming dangerously close and they could see her. Every time she put her cane down, it sparked, and made the noise B-O-N-G! So they knew that she obviously had powers. They sat there and they sat there, very still.

But *Noelhz* again couldn't keep his mouth shut. He started to snicker because *Twe-tgoi-it* obviously looked very ugly with her veil over her head.

She stopped dead in her tracks. She was disturbed. She was frightened. She stopped dead in her tracks and she looked at them. When she looked at them they became petrified. And the *Twe-tgoi-it* became petrified also. She turned into a huge mountain, and they turned into little mountains ... boulders.

Analogues

This conclusion of the adventures of the brothers seems to be unique. In all of the versions I have read, only Ken Harris mentions that the brothers turn into boulders after meeting the frightening woman with the flashing cane.

PEOPLE OF *DAMELAHAMID*

This story is used as a lesson to demonstrate the law that one should not slaughter animals needlessly. When this law is broken, punishment follows both swift and severe.

1.

Strange Feasts

The mountain goat in this story and a later one is both a destroyer and a saviour. In both cases it is a one-horned goat. It is significant that the one-horned goat who here destroys most of the people of *Damelahamid* later, in the famine story, is the instrument which saves them.

The people of *Damelahamid* lived on. The city became very large. And the people became very confident in the knowledge that they were the rulers of people and the masters of all the animals. They had many great hunters and there was so much game that hunting became a sport. They killed just for fun. They would climb the mountains and kill a mountain goat, taking very little for themselves. They would leave the dead animals to rot on the mountain sides. They would, in fact, take trophies.

One hunter, from the house of *Hagbegwatku*, was particularly a good hunter, but he would always bear in mind the instruction that they must not kill for fun; that they must only take what they needed to eat. He would take what he needed and he would spare the animals which he did not need.

One time, when a big hunt for fun was on, he went along, but he did not kill indiscriminately. He took what he needed and what his servants could carry. There was one little kid that he captured. He thought it would be nice to decorate this particular kid so that he could see it when it grew up. He wanted to mark it.

So he took his red marking and he marked the kid's face. He painted the kid's face with his red paint and he made a little cut on his head into which he stuck a feather. And he let it go. He let it go. He spared it.

At about this time, late in the fall, they had their fishing-take. This is what they would do. They would ford the river and place baskets across the river. They would control the river and they would hang baskets across it in order to trap the fish. They were able to walk on a temporary bridge across the river in order to get their fish from the traps.

At this time, one day, the children who were playing outside saw some people, obviously people of rank, come across the river. They had never seen these people before. They just knew by their appearance that they were big chiefs, great chiefs, from another village that they are pretty sure they haven't heard of because they hadn't seen these people before.

These visitors came across the river and greeted the Indians in *Damelahamid* with the usual greeting that was traditional with the people. They were taken to the chief's house. They were guests. And they said in the traditional manner that they have come to invite the people of *Damelahamid* to a feast in their village.

In the tradition of hospitality, they were fed. They were given the best type of food that the people of *Damelahamid* had to offer. Some of the servants observed that the visitors were not eating. They were just taking little bits and, instead of eating, would put the food inside their clothes. They weren't eating at all. But when the servants tried to mention this fact, they were told to mind their own place because the men were visiting dignitaries and dignitary chiefs in the olden days were treated with respect at all times and not gossiped about.

After the dinner, after all hospitality had been exhausted, the guests went out. They headed for a great big open field where the children were playing. The children were playing football, but not as rigorously as they once used to, because of the previous punishment. As they played, the visitors began to lie around on the grass. One of the children noticed that they took some food out of the clothes and that they buried it. And he called one of the bigger children and he said, "Look at what those visitors are doing! Those big chiefs are lying around. They are getting rid of all that food and, look at them, they are eating grass!"

The older children who were playing made these observations. They observed the visitors and they found that they were actually eating grass!

They went back to the chief's house and they told him, "We were playing, playing out in the field, and we noticed something very unusual about our guests. They were lying in the field and we found that they weren't eating the food. They took the food from their clothes and they buried it. They were eating the grass instead!" This was very strange for people, very strange behaviour for people.

They discussed it. They discussed it in privacy and they decided that they were not going to hurt the feelings of their guests because guests were treated with dignity. Particularly high-ranking chiefs. So they said nothing about what they had seen.

The older people, the wise people, told them, "There is something strange, something strange. You must not go. You must not go to this feast that you are summoned to. Something strange is happening here."

But the people did not heed them. They had too much respect for the visitors.

The next day they all left. The whole village went with the visitors. The villagers followed the *teeits*. They went across the river. It seemed as if they were travelling on flat land. They had no idea at all that they were climbing! They came to a village and they entered a big ceremonial house. In the big ceremonial house they noticed that the *nochnoch*, or the spirit dance, was already on. It was a one-horned goat performing in the back of the hall. They were very amused and they were very impressed. It looked so real.

They went through the complete ceremony. It was about the finest feast that they had ever attended.

The young man who was a hunter from the House of *Hagbegwatku* sat there and a young man came up to him. He was strange to look at. He had a feather in his head and his face was painted. This young man came up to him and said, "Friend, I have come to ask you to sit over there with me." The young hunter from the House of *Hagbegwatku* did not dispute the fact that he had to move from his traditional seat. All chiefs had their traditional seats and he was, after all, sitting in his own traditional seat. But somehow he had a feeling that he should not make a fuss because this strange young man had called him a friend and he had wanted him to go and sit with him. So he got up and went to sit with him in a corner.

The strange young man said, "When this is all over, everybody is going to leave, but I do not want you to move. You stay here. Don't move. You will be safe here. And I will tell you why. These people are doomed. They are being punished because they have wasted. They have wasted what was meant for them to eat. Your Father-in-Heaven is going to punish them but, because you are good, you are going to be spared. I have been sent to help you because you helped me at one time."

The one-horned mountain goat danced and danced. When this was over, except for the grand finale, they started to sing:

> Haw eh yaw,
> Haw ehyaw haha,
> Haw eh yaw,
> Haw ehyaw haha,
> Haw eh yaw,
> Haw ehyaw ha ha . . .

and while they were singing this, two mountain goats appeared at a time. The guests from *Damelahamid* thought that they were *nochnochs*; that their hosts were imitating animals as physical signs of *nochnochs*. They looked so real that the guests were very impressed. The goats would appear from different

48

sides of the building and they would criss-cross and disappear into the corners while the people were singing and chanting.

Finally, the hunter from the House of *Hagbegwatku* saw his strange young friend with the painted face leave. The one-horned goat appeared again and danced. He danced to the point where people were just hypnotized and then he went to one corner. He kicked the corner and the corner just shook. He went to another corner and he kicked it and that corner just shook. He kicked all the four corners and the corners shook. Then he danced again. He danced and he disappeared into a corner.

There was nobody left! The *tdo-a* looked at each other and decided that their hosts had all gone and it was time to leave. "What a strange way to end it," they thought. It was time to go. So they started to go out the door one by one and they left. They disappeared.

The young man from the House of *Hagbegwatku* didn't move. He stayed there as he had been instructed to do by his friend. When daylight came, he found that he was sitting right in the heart of the mountains, at *tse kho don*. He found himself sitting there. He looked around. Lo and behold, he saw dead bodies scattered all over the place. He was very sad. He was sitting there when he heard his friend's voice.

"I have come. I have come for you now. But you notice what has happened. It was a punishment because they have wasted. And," he said, "this is what I am going to have to do. I am going to have to lend you my coat because you won't be able to get down this mountainside without my feet." And he gave him instructions. He said, "You are going to jump from one rock to the other, and where there is no rock you are to say *'Koelhz se mos'*. When you say *'Koelhz se mos,'* you will see what happens."

So he put on his friend's coat. He became a mountain goat and he started to go down the mountainside. When he ran out of places to step on, he said, *"Koelhz se mos"* and a little boulder just appeared in front of him as something for him to step on. He went down the hill that way, saying *"Koelhz se mos," "Koelhz se mos," "Koelhz se mos,"* until he got to the bottom. His friend was right behind him. When they got to the bottom he gave his friend back his coat and they parted. He knew now that it was the little kid which he had once spared that had come back to help him.

He returned to *Damelahamid* and told the sad story. He told the sad story and the elders said, "We had a feeling that something like this was going to happen. That is why we forbade you to take heed of this invitation."

They were all very sad. But they knew they had done something wrong and that their Father-in-Heaven in traditional fashion had punished them again. He had punished them before, and again they were punished.

Analogues

Boas cites three Tsimshian and Kwakiutl versions of "The Feast of the Mountain Goats."[1] In one recorded from the Kwakiutl the principal mountain goat has one horn. In a Tsimshian version, the children mistreat a kid by throwing it into the water and then into fire. It is rescued by a young man, who is the one person saved when, at a later feast, a one-horned goat destroys a house and causes everyone else to be killed by a rock-slide. The man jumps down the mountain saying, "On the thumb!" and "On the sand!" He then burns the bones of the goats which have been left lying around by the villagers and revives his relatives. In both the Boas Tsimshian version and that of Ken Harris, the story of the one-horned goat directly follows that of the feather.

In Will Robinson's collected stories, "The Little Goat," "L-La-Matte," "The Feast," and "The Law," the same theme is treated.[2] The kid is

---

[1] Boas, *Tsimshian Mythology*, p. 131; notes, p. 738.
[2] Robinson, *Men of Medeek*, pp. 5-15.

50

tortured by fire and is rescued by a "man of the common people." He carries his ruler's regalia up to the feast on *Stekyawden*. A one-horned goat dances, tilting the large house. Leaving, the guests fall over a cliff and are killed. As the poor wise man is led to safety by a kid, he wears the little goat's blanket and utters the words "sand slope" as he descends. The moral is stated in "The Law"; to take in sport the life that *Gyamk* (the sun god) gave is forbidden. In Ken Harris's version, the elders of *Damelahamid* are left alive in order to point out the moral to the surviving hunter.

2.

The Flood

This introduces *Way deetai* who is said to have had a *hawlhz-ganku* from which he fed all the people on the *dakh*. It is the second time a *hawlhz-ganku* makes its appearance. Ken Harris holds the title of *Way deetai* as his personal *nochnoch*. The name-title, *Way deetai*, belongs to Gordon Smith of Hazelton. The *nochnochs* remain in the House of *Hagbegwatku*. The Prime Minister of Canada, the Honourable Pierre Elliot Trudeau, was given an honorary *Way deetai* title when he visited Prince Rupert in 1970. The significance of *Way deetai* feeding all of the people from an apparently bottomless box should not be missed.

The rainbow appears on the blankets of the people of *Damelahamid*. The Speaker of the House, *Hanamok*, and another of *Hagbegwatku*'s brothers, *Nagwa*, also use it as their personal crests.

The *dakh* in this story landed on the mountain behind Kispiox, on a spot called *Wissinskid*. A second *dakh* landed behind *Spokehōd*, now known as Port Essington, and the people of the coast, the Tsimshians, came from this *dakh*. The third *dakh* broke loose and disappeared in the storm. We have no idea where it went. Regarding this third *dakh*, Ken Harris tells a story: "I was very surprised when I was on the National Advisory Board to the Indian Affairs Branch, when I ran into some people from the Six Nations. They were Hurons. I met a Hereditary Chief. We discussed the difference between Hereditary Chiefs and elected chiefs after the order of the Indian Act that was created by the Indian Affairs Branch. He told me that he was the Householder of his clan. He spoke of the long house and his matriarchal mother, and I told him the story of the missing *dakh*. He said that there was no one who recalled exactly their origin. His appearance was different from the Prairie Indians. He was more like our Northwest Coast Indians of *Damelahamid*. His clan was the Turtle Clan, but I realized that this was because of the different type of animals in Ontario. I have an idea that the third *dakh* might have drifted into that area."

There are other people who tell us today how they survived the Flood. The Nass people claim they survived on the top of a mountain. The Squamish people tell us that they survived by tying many canoes together.

Time went on and *Damelahamid* became a huge city again. People became so many that neighbours did not know neighbours. They say that when birds flew over the city the people out on the streets would shout, causing them to panic. They flew over and the people would shout and the birds would fly so hard that they got exhausted, and before they came to the end of the city, they would fall in exhaustion. That was how big *Damelahamid* was.

The people became very confident again. All of a sudden it started to rain.

It started to rain and the shores of the water changed. The water came up. It kept coming up and it did not stop raining. The people recalled the instructions that had been given to them, handed down to them from generation to generation. They recalled that their Father-in-Heaven who had brought them there and put them in *Damelahamid* had told them that the face of the earth would be washed and that they were not to run away.

As soon as some people saw the water rising, the ocean rising, they took their families and sought the highlands. They went to the tops of mountains. But the people of *Damelahamid*, who had been given instructions, did exactly what they had been instructed to do.

They had three *dakhs* at this time, but they only had one *gilhast*. One *gilhast*. They cut it down according to instruction. They cut it down and they fortified their *dakhs* with it. They fortified them and when the water came they felt very secure and relaxed.

There was a time when they weren't sure. They nearly packed up and left when, all of a sudden, a strange person appeared in their midst. They looked at him. He was obviously one of them because he spoke their language. He said to them, "Don't be afraid. Don't run away. You have done what you have been instructed. You will remain on your *dakhs*." The stranger was speaking on the chief's *dakh, Hagbegwatku's dakh*.

They called the stranger *Way deetai* because of his appearance. His hair was light in colour and his eyes were a very light brown.

The water rose and the three *dakhs* started to float and they anchored them. They had made anchor ropes. They made them from combined hide and roots and barks of trees. They had made them and stock-piled them. They were very long ropes. And they were anchored. Each *dakh* was anchored and they were all fortified by the *gilhast*.

Now the water rose and rose and they floated away. They floated and they were anchored. It is told that it was a whole year from the time it started to rain until, one day, they observed that there were two rainbows in the sky.

Before this time all the birds had flocked to the air where they had nowhere to rest. The sky was just crowded with birds and the birds, in their exhaustion, started to shed their feathers. The top of the waters became very thick with feathers. The people of *Damelahamid* who were on the three *dakhs* observed this. They observed also, after a year's time, that two rainbows appeared in the sky. As the rainbows touched the surface of the waters full of feathers, the water started to recede. It started to go down.

When the land started to appear again, they first of all recognized their hunting ground where they used to hunt for groundhogs. And they made a lament. They lamented. They lamented because they recognized their own country. They weren't very far from where *Damelahamid* was.

They made their chant and they took the rainbow and it became one of their coats-of-arms. The rainbows were a sign that the waters were going to recede.

After the *dakh* landed, they made a litter. They made a litter for their chief. They became very close to God again, to their Father-in-Heaven. They became very close to their Creator again, and they felt that their chief was a direct descendant of their God. They made a litter so that he would not have to walk. And the litter was all veiled over and they carried him. They carried him back to *Damelahamid* their city; the city that was given to them.

They rebuilt. They built some *dakhs* again. They had been told that there was only going to be one flood, but they were not assured. They built *dakhs* again in the same traditional form that they had built them before.

They got another tall pole with absolutely no features on it and they erected it again in front of their chief's house, the House of *Hagbegwatku*. They erected the *gilhast*. They settled.

After all the people had returned to *Damelahamid* they reconstructed the village. *Way deetai* was still with them. He was the strange person who had appeared in the *dakh* at the beginning of the flood. He said, "I am going to go to look for possible survivors." And he did.

Analogues

Boas recorded two Tsimshian versions of "The Deluge,"[1] a theme which is recognized world-wide. Because the people of *T!Emlax'ā'm* mistreated a trout, rain sets in for twenty days. The anchor-lines of the canoes break and the people drift. Some climb mountains and are drowned as the earth becomes submerged. As the waters settle, the people live wherever they have drifted. "In this manner the crests are scattered over the whole coast." After the Flood, one version states that there is only clay left, no trees, and the people live in tents. The other myth states that mountains originated during the Deluge. In the Ken Harris version, some of the people returned to *Damelahamid* with their new hero *Way deetai* who is still with them.

---

[1] Boas, *Tsimshian Mythology*, p. 113; notes, p. 727.

3.

The Medeek

The *hegee* mentioned in this story translates as an "instrument for killing." It is larger than a tomahawk and there are very few of them left. The only one that Ken Harris has seen was in Alaska. The *hegee* in the story was the only one made in *Damelahamid*.

There is a lament that tells of the *medeek* surfacing and of the movements of the *medeek* as it came ashore. The *medeek* became another symbol of the House of *Hagbegwatku*, a constant reminder of this story and the exploits of *Tso ech* and *Yabadets*.

The people had returned to *Damelahamid* and had reconstructed it. They started to flourish. They started to flourish in large numbers. They found that *Damelahamid* was no longer on the shores of the big ocean.

They found that the ocean was no longer at the doorsteps of *Damelahamid*. Before the flood, the shores of the ocean were right up to *Damelahamid* and it wasn't until after the flood that the tidal waters receded down the river.

They found that there were now several lakes. There were lakes all over. They found that water, running water, was plentiful. There was running water from all the little lakes and ponds that were created by the big flood. Any little hollow capable of containing water, retained the water and became a lake. One of the lakes was not far from *Damelahamid*. They called it *Mean tse kho don*, meaning base of the mountain. Now it was said that a huge monster of a bear, with the appearance of a bear with brown-gold skin, lived in this lake. The lake was land-locked. The Indians said, *"Lo gin a gwelk."* It was a sea-monster. The monster had apparently been known before the flood and was now land-locked in this little lake, *Mean tse kho don.*

The lake had a lot of trout in it. It was just full of trout and there were nice berry-picking grounds all around it. The shores were lined with berries, blueberries. The young people of *Damelahamid* would go there to pick the berries. It was habitual for them to go there, especially the young ladies. Their servants would go and pick berries at *Mean tse kho don.* And they all started to do something very foolish.

They started to do something very foolish. They would catch all kinds of trout and they took the bones with the tails still on them and made head-dresses of them. They made head-dresses and they danced. They danced in the moonlight. In the moonlight, the tails of the trout sparkled and dazzled on their heads as they moved about, dancing.

They enjoyed doing this and it got to the point that they caught the trout just for the sake of making head-dresses. They enjoyed themselves.

And the monster, the *medeek*, would surface. He surfaced and he killed all the people. He killed all of them who didn't get away. People would try to kill the *medeek*. They tried to surround it and kill it with bows and arrows. They couldn't. They left their arrows in the skin, sticking out. They couldn't kill it.

One time they were picking berries again. One of the chief's nieces, her name was *Tshā get she lā*, went with the berry-picking party. They picked the berries, and they did the same thing. They repeated the foolish act; they danced and they used trout bones as head-dresses. There was much laughing and gaiety. They were enjoying themselves very much.

The *medeek* surfaced and killed them. And *Tshā get she lā* was slain, was slain by the *medeek*.

The servants returned to *Damelahamid* and told them what had happened. *Tshā get she lā* was slain. She had two brothers,

Tso ech and *Yabadets*. They were both warriors. They were both very brave warriors, trained in the art of battle, trained in the art of killing. They decided they were going to kill the *medeek*.

They went back to the lake and they used servants and slaves to entice the *medeek* out. They watched him carefully. They watched every move that he made. They saw that when he stood up on his hind legs he would lift his arms. They knew that it was very, very tender under his arms. They decided how they were going to kill the *medeek*.

They made a *hegee*. They made very strong arrows, bows and arrows, and they dug themselves a trench. They dug a trench and they hid themselves in this. They made the servants dance to entice the *medeek* out of the lake, while they were prepared to kill it in a counter-attack.

Finally, it surfaced again. It surfaced. It came ashore.

The *medeek* came up on the shore. All the people who were there shot at it with arrows. The arrows didn't stop it. It kept coming.

Meanwhile, *Tso ech* and *Yabadets* hid themselves in the trench so that they could attack the *medeek* at close quarters. When it came right up on top of them *Tso ech*, with his bow and arrow, jumped up from his trench and shot the *medeek* in the tender part of its armpit. The *medeek* went down. It didn't die. It went down temporarily. It got up again, but it got up too quickly. *Tso ech* shot him again. He shot him again in the other armpit and the *medeek* went down.

This time *Yabadets* went after the *medeek* with the *hegee* and he got him. He hit him right on the forehead with the *hegee*, and the *medeek* was slain. It was killed.

They cut the *medeek*'s head off and they showed it to the people of *Damelahamid*. They lamented. They chanted that they had slain the *medeek*, the man-killer that had slain their sister. They had avenged their sister. They showed the *medeek* to the people. They took the hide.

They took it back to their chief, Chief *Hagbegwatku*, and he made a blanket out of it, his own personal blanket. He left the broken arrows in it showing that it took many arrows and many sacrifices to slay the *medeek*, the enemy of the people.

But they all soon realized that this was no common enemy of the people. It was a warning. They had been warned again. They had been punished again because they were foolish. They had played with the fishes from the water. They had not taken the fish for something to eat. They used the fish to amuse themselves.

Hagbegwatku took the hide with the arrows still in it. There were seating arrangements in his house. The chief sat right in the centre of the house and the other chiefs of the household, chiefs of his clan, had places on either side of him in order of priority. In order of importance. *Hagbegwatku* sat in the centre, wearing his blanket. When he got too crowded, he would move around. He moved around and the arrows that were in the hide would poke at the people sitting beside him, forcing them to move away. They were forced to move away, giving him more room. And thus the name of the blanket was born — it was called *givees lootsen gues*, "make more room for himself." He did this on purpose because he wanted room at the very centre of the house, because he was the householder, the chief of all the people of *Damelahamid*, the chief of all the clans.

Analogues

In Will Robinson's collection, Walter Wright's recounting of "The Vengeance of Medeek"[1] parallels the preceding Ken Harris story. The lake is nestled near the foot of Mount *Stekyawden*. The story is more

[1] Robinson, *Men of Medeek*, p. 16.

detailed than the Harris one and apparently takes place over a longer time span. Instead of the *medeek* surfacing and killing the dancing people decked in trout bones near the lake, the giant grizzly bear makes his way, tearing great trees out of the earth, to the town of *Tum-L-Hama*. "That battle ground was three miles long. The bear moved from house to house, killing all who opposed him." He finally returned to the forest and the lake, leaving a trail of destruction and desolation. In Wright's following story "The Grizzly Bears,"[2] the wise men realize that their people have offended *Gyamk*, the sun god, in desecrating the trout. New laws, governing the proper training of children, were introduced and the head of the *medeek*, the Grizzly Bear, became the crest of the Totem of *Neas Hiwas*, the chief, and his men became known as the Men of Medeek.

[2] Ibid., p. 20.

MOVE TO *KITSEKUCLA*

This story illustrates the law that one does not taunt the Heavenly Father or flaunt one's goods in His face. When this law is broken, punishment follows both swift and severe.

1.

The Big Snowfall

Deelepzeb means "His own city." It is a leading name, given to a prince who is destined to be the chief of *Damelahamid*. This name was passed to Ken Harris when he was a young boy. It was also his first title.

The lament sung by the two sisters is still sung when the Indians lament the death of any of their people. It tells how the girls found the little piece of fish which might have saved their starving brother.

It happened in the springtime. They had already forded the river and put out their fish traps. They were going to trap the salmon as the salmon run came up the river. When they checked their traps they found there were several spring salmon in them. They took the spring salmon home to the chief's house.

As was customary in those days, the chief prepared the first catch of the season and he fed the whole city. This is what happened. He prepared the spring salmon and cut them up into pieces and cooked them. He prepared them and put them on platters. And the servants and the princesses and the princes of the house went from house to house delivering cooked food — the first catch of the season.

While they were doing this, a hailstorm happened. It hailed. One of the princes of *Damelahamid* was named *Deelepzeb*. *Deelepzeb* had a platter of salmon and he looked up into the heavens. He knew that that was where his Father was, and he felt that he was very close to Him because, according to history, he was the direct descendant of his Heavenly Father. He looked up into the sky and he said, "Just what is the meaning of this?

63

Hail in the middle of summer? Look at what we have already. We have already got spring salmon. What sort of nonsense is this that it should hail at this time?"

There was no more thought of it. They delivered their salmon but several people had heard him and thought it was a foolish thing to do. To taunt your Heavenly Father was foolish, and *Deelepzeb* had done just this.

That night it started to snow. The weather changed and it started to freeze. It snowed so deeply that they couldn't walk and the river, the *Kshian*, froze so that the people couldn't fish. It was frozen. They couldn't go up in the bush to hunt because there was so much snow and the weather was so bad. And because it was springtime, they had used up all their provisions. They did not have very much left.

They began to run into real problems. They had no food left and people started to starve. They starved by the thousands.

They were dying.

Two sisters, *Deelepzeb*'s sisters, thought of their favourite hunting grounds further down the river at *Kitsekucla*. One sister was *Nege-elhz* and the other was called *Siggite looks*. They thought of *Dahemgeest* where they usually fished for trout. So they took their brother who was already ailing, sick from hunger, and put him on a sleigh. They put him on the *ahk hkai-hō* and they pulled him down the river on the ice. They were able to walk on the ice, it was so thick.

They went a long way and then they camped. Their brother couldn't go any further. He was feeling very sick. They had nothing to give him. They had run out of food. And he died. He died of starvation.

They burned him, and, after the tradition, they burned his things with him. While they were burning him, a little parcel fell out of his belongings. They opened this parcel and they found it was half a dried fish — half a dried salmon. They were very sad. They were very sad and they lamented.

They took the fish and they cut it into small pieces and ate it. They ate just a little at a time, just to keep them going. They began to look around. But what could they do? They couldn't see anything. There was nothing around. The snow was very deep. There was ice on the river. Everything was frozen over.

Finally, they ran out of food. They started to go downstream again, down the *Kshian*. Suddenly they felt heat, heat-waves coming on the wind. It was blowing in their faces. It was heat! They couldn't understand it. They thought the weather must be changing.

They walked faster. And they came to the edge of the winter's snow. They found that it was already summer. Summer was nearly over. They looked around and they found out that the snow area was only within the limits of *Damelahamid*. They realized then that they had been punished again.

They realized that the people had been punished because of the foolish youngster who had taunted his Heavenly Father.

They looked around. They found a wild crab-apple on the rose-bush. They took it. It was getting fairly ripe as summer was almost over. They broke it in half and *Siggite looks* ate half of it and gave the other half to her sister, *Nege-elhz*. They made up another lament telling of how they came across the little crab-apple and broke it in half and ate it for survival.

Analogues

Boas mentions eight versions from Tsimshian, Tlingit, Haida, Chilcotin, Shuswap and Kathlamet sources.[1] In his Tsimshian story, a woman and her husband are the sole survivors. They travel down river after seeing a bluejay holding a ripe cluster of elderberries. All of the other versions also mention a bird carrying a type of berry. The woman catches trout, thus saving her starving husband. They discover another group of people, and the husband marries into the new tribe. Wherever these new people moved, there was a heavy snowdrift on the ground.

[1] Boas, *Tsimshian Mythology*, p. 250; notes, p. 829.

2.

Adventures of Two Sisters

Unlike the story of *Strange Feasts*, the one-horned goat in this story is not an instrument of destruction but a saviour.

While the two sisters were making up their new lament they heard a drumming noise. It came from a little grouse sitting on a log. They crept up and saw it. It was a grouse, sitting on a log, drumming its little heart out. They made a plan to try to catch it for food.

They crept up to the grouse on their stomachs but they could not get close enough. The little grouse disappeared. They sat down and thought. They decided to dig holes on each side of the log in which both of them would hide. This they did.

They made a trench on both sides of the log and they lay down in them. They stuck their arms up on the sides of the log where the little grouse had sat and drummed. They covered their arms with moss so that the grouse would not be afraid. They waited for a long time and finally the grouse appeared. It sat on the log and it came so close to *Siggite looks* that she grabbed it. She got hold of its tail and the whole tail structure came out. It fell out and the grouse got away.

They sat there and they thought. They decided that something had to be done. So they made snares and they put them on the log and they waited. Finally, the little drummer came back. They snared the grouse and caught it. They caught it by the feet.

They lived off the grouse and this gave them a little more time. Then they remembered that they had to get to the lake, *Dahemgeest*, where they had always caught trout. They got to the lake but they found that there was still ice on it. They could not do anything. They had nothing. They had no tools to cut through ice.

So they got some rocks. They got several big rocks and they started a fire and they put the rocks on the fire. When a rock became red hot they carried it down to the lake and put it on one spot on the ice. They took turns. They kept replacing the rock as it cooled off with a hot rock. To speed things up, they took the ashes from the fire and carried them down in bark from cedar trees. They carried the ashes down and sometimes they got spilt. This made a track of ashes going from the fire to the rocks on the ice. It was almost like a stream of ashes. So they gave the name of *tse-lahad-hū* to this particular part of the lake. It means "where ashes were split."

They kept putting the hot rocks on one spot of the ice until finally, the heat broke through. The heat ate a hole in the ice. They looked into the hole and they saw trout — many trout — and they were happy. They had a hole in the ice and there were trout.

They set about very quickly and made tools for catching trout. These were little nets on handles. They wove separated roots from trees into little nets or little baskets on the ends of poles and they caught trout. They caught many trout through the hole in the ice, and they started to smoke the fish. They were thinking of their people back in *Damelahamid*. They thought of how hungry their people must be by now and wondered how many had died from hunger.

While they were sitting there, smoking the trout, they looked up at the mountain. They saw a mountain goat. They thought of the story that was told of the mountain goats that retaliated when the people mistreated them. The goat on the mountain they were watching only had one horn in the middle of its head.

They said, "We will have to go up and catch this goat. It means survival." They made ropes from bark and tree roots and they made many snares. They climbed up the mountain. They found the different paths that the mountain goat used and they set their snares on the paths. Then they went down to the lake and sat down and waited.

Eventually they saw the one-horned goat re-appear and they waited. They waited very impatiently and finally saw it go through one of the snares and trip. It tripped and they watched the goat hang dangling, tossing about. Now they were very happy. They were very happy and made a new chant.

Then they went up the mountain, took the mountain goat and dried it. By this time they had a lot of food — goat and smoked dried trout. They started to gather their things and took what they could carry and returned to *Damelahamid*.

Analogues

Nothing in the major sources parallels the foregoing Ken Harris story. In none of the eight versions of the Boas story "Local Winter in G-IT-Q!Ā' " are there similar adventures.[1] It is interesting to note his reference to a one-horned goat. Boas also mentions one-horned mountain goats playing an important part in Kwakiutl mythology as either a chief or a chief's messenger among the Goats.[2]

---

[1] Boas, *Tsimshian Mythology*, p. 250; notes, p. 829.
[2] Ibid., p. 738.

3.

Moving of Many People

The frog is the clan crest of the *Ganadda* phratry. Their chief was called *Ghuldeg hed*.

S*iggite looks* and *Nege-elhz* returned to *Damelahamid* with all their food. They found that there were very few people left. Most of them were very hungry and were dying of starvation. They fed some of the servants and some of the people and the food gave them strength.

The two sisters went back to the lake and got the rest of the food. Back in *Damelahamid*, they rationed it to the people. They were afraid that some people might eat too much, and then they would die. The people got strength from the food and *Siggite looks* and *Nege-elhz* told the chief, their uncle, what had happened and what they had found. They told him about their brother, *Deelepzeb*, and they lamented. They all lamented because the title prince had died.

The people decided then, after they had held council, that they were going to leave *Damelahamid*, the promised city, the city that their Creator had given to them. They were punished because they had done something that they were not supposed to do. They felt that they had had enough punishment. They decided to leave *Damelahamid*, and leave it they did. They packed their belongings and they went down the river.

They moved to *Kitsekucla* and established a new city there. Everyone moved and built new houses, many new houses. But all shared the history of *Damelahamid* and the exploits. They shared everything as do brothers.

And it was told that another phratry — *Ganadda* phratry — lived across the river from *Damelahamid* (where Hazelton is now located). The chief was called *Ghuldeg hed*, *Hed* for short. *Hed* had a big house and a big family. They all respected *Hed* and they liked him. This was the rule. The people of *Damelahamid* respected *Hed* because it was the ethics of the people that they had to respect their opposition.

Hed had a great big door on his house. At night, when he closed the door, it could be heard. The door went "bang — whoooop!" The people of *Damelahamid* would say, "*Hed* has closed his door. He is going to bed, and so will we all." And they would. They had a lot of respect for one another.

Analogues

In the *Men of Medeek*, Walter Wright tells of the migratory wanderings of the people following times of famine. However, Ken Harris's version was the only one to mention a definite move to the area known as Kitsegucla.

4.

Lo-tres-kū's Story

Ken Harris had permission from Chief *Laelt* who succeeded his grandfather, Solomon Harris, to tell the story of the mother of the Raven clan.
The story belongs in this place as it is also of *Hed*'s people. The matriarch
of the Ravens is called *Lo-tres-kū*.

The *medeek* mentioned is not that of the previous story. This one was
swimming in Hecate Strait and was called the *Medeekum hatl wap*.

The names that the Raven clan of the *Ganadda* phratry have in their
House today all originate from *Lo-tres-kū*'s experiences. The tying of the
baby's loins with hair is a name. Soothing the baby with the tongue of his
dead father is another name. The bird which flew over the canoe, showing
the way, is another. And, as she went up the Nass River by mistake
another name was born.

The man-made hill exists today. It is called *Da ochems*. On one of the
totem poles of the Raven clan there are flat people who were crushed by
logs rolling down this hill. These are the *Haida*. The pole belongs to the
House of *Laelt*.

H*ed* took his family and also moved to the new site
of *Kitsekucla*. They also built houses and claimed land.

However, there was a battle. There was a raid from the
Tsimshians. Warriors came up the *Kshian*. They captured a
young Indian princess from Kitwanga. Her name was *Lo-tres-
kū*. They carried her downstream and they put her up for
auction. She was for sale.

A chief from the *Haidah* people, named *Awāk*, saw that she
was a princess, so he bought her to be his wife. He took her to
the Queen Charlotte Islands or *La Haidah*. She had children.

71

She had a son the first time. The servants took the son to its father, *Awāk*. *Awāk* looked at his son and he was afraid. He was scared because of the nature of things. His wasn't a marriage in the traditional fashion, but a marriage-by-purchase, and he was afraid that his son would retaliate after the order of the system and kill him when he grew up. He pretended that he loved his new son, but what he actually did was to put his tongue over the baby's mouth and nose and smothered it. He returned it to his mother, dead.

A second son was born. The same thing happened. *Awāk* killed the child. He did not want a son because he was afraid his son would retaliate and free his mother from a condition of captivity.

The third time a son was born, *Awāk*'s own relatives, who were very fond of their sister-in-law, made a plan. They told her that they were going to fix the baby boy so that it would look like a girl. They braided hair — they cut their own hair off — and they took the boy and disguised him. They wrapped their hair around his loins and they took him to his father, *Awāk*. They said, "Look! This time you have a girl!" *Awāk* looked at the baby and said, "Fine! This girl will live." He returned the baby to his mother.

The child was returned to his mother who had remained in seclusion in an enclosure made for this purpose. Soon, however, the mother would have to come out and show the baby to the people. *Awāk*'s relatives made a plan. They told *Lo-tres-kū*, "We have arranged for you to escape. We have a canoe. Tonight, you must escape. The people will run after you and try to catch you. You must not go very far. You must hide your canoe and you will wait. You must count all the canoes that go past you."

So *Lo-tres-kū* did this. That evening, she kept her husband awake. She had had a lot of sleep herself, but she kept her husband awake. Finally, late at night, he went to sleep and she took a knife and cut his head off. She took the child and the knife and *Awāk*'s head down to the canoe and got in and

72

started to paddle. The baby started to cry. She could not stop to feed the child, so she sharpened a stick and pulled *Awāk's* tongue out of his head and stuck the stick through it. She then put *Awāk's* tongue in the baby's mouth. It kept the child quiet while she was paddling.

Soon, she pulled her canoe up on the beach and covered it with leaves. She erased any sign of tracks. In the morning, she saw many canoes, heading in her direction. She counted every one of them. Towards evening, she counted the same number of canoes returning. They had decided to look in the opposite direction.

After all the canoes had returned, she took her canoe and her child and they crossed Hecate Strait. They were heading for what is now known as Kitwanga. She paddled and paddled.

While she was paddling, a very strange bird flew over the top of her and she adopted it as her insignia. Then a very strange animal appeared. It was a *medeek*. She adopted the *medeek* that she saw also and it became her clan crest. She called it the *Medeekum hatl wap*.

The *medeek* did not capsize her canoe. It did not bother her. Instead, it seemed to bless her and escorted her, keeping her from harm. She was very thankful. She felt that the *medeek* helped her escape. The *medeek* surfaced and just put its paws on the edge of the canoe, but it did not rock it.

Lo-tres-kū missed the mouth of the Skeena River and went up the Nass River by mistake.

As she paddled up the Nass River, her relatives living there recognized her. They took her in. They looked after her through the winters and her son grew. When her son was quite grown up, he took her back to the Skeena River and Kitwanga.

In the meantime, the people of *La Haidah* had learned that *Lo-tres-kū* had returned. They decided to make war against her people. They came over in hordes. *Lo-tres-kū* was ready for them, however. She ordered a hill built, a man-made hill. All her warriors were on top of the hill. They had surrounded the hill with big logs. They were tied and ready to roll down the hill.

Sentries were posted in trenches waiting with deer hoofs and things to sound the alarm.

The people of *La Haidah* came in hordes. They surrounded the hill. They wanted to climb the hill quickly and destroy the few people at the top. When the *Haidah* were half up the mountain, the guards pulled the strings and the signal was given by the rattling of the deer hoofs. When the warriors on the top heard this, they cut the logs loose and they rolled down the hill, killing all the *Haidah* warriors.

THE ORIGIN OF THE THUNDERBIRD, *TWE TJEA-ADKU*

This story is told to demonstrate the distaste which occurs following incest, underlying the essential rule of exogamous marriage in order for the matrilineal system to survive. When this law is broken, punishment follows, both swift and severe.

Every story that the Indians hand down by word to their children is usually expressed in a form that would be attractive to them to understand. In the olden days, the punishment for incest was death.

The Origin of the Thunderbird, Twe tjea-adku

The Thunderbird is found as one of the crests from all the people who originated in *Damelahamid*. The Tsimshian, Nishga, Haidas, Kwakiutls, and Tlingits all have it. Because of the extraordinary way the Thunderbird came into being, it became a *nochnoch* known as *Twe tjea-adku*. Today, when the Indians hear thunder, they mock it and shout, "You are having incest with your sister!"

It is told that, during the time of *Damelahamid*, there lived there a chief who became attracted by the sister of *Hagbegwatku* who was the chief of *Damelahamid*. According to the rituals, they were married.

So *Hagbegwatku*'s sister married a chief of another clan and a boy was born to this woman. Not too long after, they had another child and this time it was a girl. The chief was very fond of his children and the two were instructed to love one another as only done by brothers and sisters. They shared everything they had. When they went to play, they played together.

In those days, a prince and a princess of the house had a special arrangement where they slept. They slept on what is known as a *tyak tyak* which was a balcony at the head of the house. They shared a bed and also in keeping with tradition, they had servants to sleep at the bottom of the ladder. If they wanted anything in the middle of the night, their servants would wait on them. The servants also acted as guards for the young people.

Days passed and the two children became older and stronger.

They went together to get their food, their berries, as it was a tradition that a prince and princess were not allowed to become lazy or useless. They went with their servants and did the amount of manual labour expected of them. They organized the picking of berries and the gathering of food for the long winter months to come. They did this together.

Their father, the chief, was very pleased with them, and their uncle, Chief *Hagbegwatku*, was very pleased with them. For a long period of time, no one paid too much attention to the growing affection between the two youngsters. When they became older, they were inseparable. They refused to be separated. Everywhere they went, they went together. They could not live without each other.

Their mother became suspicious. The two had now entered young adulthood, and their mother found out that their brotherly love for each other had developed into another form of affection. She was very disappointed. She carried her secret with her long enough to know that she had discovered the truth about her children.

Finally, she took her husband into her confidence and told him what had transpired between the two young people. They had found love with one another beyond that between brothers and sisters. They had become *kaitz* which was forbidden among the clanspeople. When the mother confided in her husband, the chief, he became very sad. He called together all his relatives and all his wife's relatives, including Chief *Hagbegwatku* of *Damelahamid*. They were all very fond of the two children. They knew that the ultimate punishment was death and they did not want to see this happen. In order to evade passing judgment, the council of chiefs decided that whatever their father decided to do would be sufficient. They could not bear to pass judgment on the two youngsters.

The father decided to make an example of his two children. He ordered that a platform be built in front of his house, high enough above the heads of the people so that everyone could see the two on it. It was built. He also ordered that all his people go out and kill all types of birds and bring back the feathers to him. Many different types of beautiful birds were slain and many different types of feathers were brought to him. He ordered his servants to go out and collect pitch from the trees. They softened the pitch and prepared it.

The day came when he called the people of the city of *Damelahamid* to bear witness to the punishment bestowed on his two children. They were put on the platform and stripped naked. They were shaved bald and the pitch was applied to their bodies. Feathers were placed on the pitch. They were left sitting on the platform so that everyone could see them. It was a lesson to everyone of the harm that had been done by their relationship.

Their mother had a box, a utility box, in which all her utensils, or *no-elhz*, were stored. The box was called a *hawlhz-ganku*. She ordered her servant to place the box beside her daughter who was already on display on the platform.

Many days passed. People went by the platform and looked up at the two young people. Some shouted "scandalous!" at them and called them *kaitz*. Then one day the people heard a noise of thunder. They heard a series of thunder-like noises and they went outside. They found that the two young people had changed in appearance. They still wore feathers and they had started to flap their arms as if they were birds. Their facial expressions had changed. Their heads began to look more like birds than humans. When they flapped their arms, the people heard a loud rolling noise.

Soon the two were able to fly. By flapping their arms which now looked like wings, they were able to fly. The young girl picked up the *hawlz-ganku* and flew as high as she could. She started to empty the box. She took out the *no-elhz* one by one and threw them down at the people who were jeering. The people were looking up at them and were jeering and calling them *kaitz*. When the dishes or *no-elhz* landed, lightning struck at that spot. When the box was empty, the two flew so high that they disappeared.

But every so often, they were seen. Whenever they were seen, there was a thunder-like noise. And this was the origin of the Thunderbird.

THE ORIGIN OF THE KILLER WHALE

This story demonstrates war conditions existing between mankind, the animal kingdom, and the supernatural. It illustrates how clan crests are established.

1.

Gudeloch and the Princess

The Killer Whale is a secondary crest of Ken Harris's clan, but it is a very popular one. They were first known as the People of the *hast* — the *Gisgahast* — or the Fireweed people.

The box in this story is a utility box and is known as a *gelink*. It is not a *hawlhz-ganku*. All the utility and storage boxes were marked by a design typical of their particular House, showing where the owner originated. The design was the House crest.

Ken Harris says that his people traditionally tell of help that is brought by little field mice.

Note that this story occurs *before* the Flood.

I t is told that during the time of *Damelahamid* before the flood, the ocean reached the shores of *Damelahamid*, right up to what is now the Skeena River. There lived in *Damelahamid* a chief who had a sister with a young daughter of marriageable age. She had not yet been married. Everyone was very proud of this young girl.

The women used to travel far away from the village to gather berries, particularly the salmonberries which they used to pick around the area on the coastline where *Stekyawden* is today. One day, a party of young girls left to pick berries at *Stekyawden* and the young princess went with them. During the day they had a very good time picking berries. All the young girls helped the princess to pick berries and filled her box.

The boxes were filled and it became time to journey back, so they started. The young princess was very happy. She was very happy that she had participated in the berry-picking for the day. She did not notice that in the path was a large deposit of bear waste. It was quite fresh. She stepped on it and slipped. Her berries were scattered all over the ground and she became very sad. The young girls picked up her box and the berries that were on the top and not dirty. They filled up her box again to the original level by taking some of their own berries and they helped her on her way again.

She hadn't gone very far when her carrying strap or *tgadlech* broke. This was unusual as they had been tested. They were very strong and made from young, fresh wool. The same thing happened. The box fell and the berries fell all over the ground. She was very sad and again her young friends helped her repack her box. They were close to the city of *Damelahamid* now so she said to them, "There is no use me wasting your time any more. You haven't too far to go. I will sit here and wait. You go into the city and tell my brothers to come and help me. I will just sit here and wait for them."

They left her. They hadn't gone very long when she noticed that her two brothers had come to fetch her. But they were behaving very strangely. Instead of picking up the box and tying the carrying straps, they ate what was in the box very rapidly. They ate everything, and she was quite dismayed by this, but she didn't say anything. They were her brothers. When they were finished, they broke her box. They slapped it and it broke. They said, "Oh, don't worry about that. We will make you another one. Come with us now. We haven't got too much time." She couldn't say anything. She was obedient to the wishes of her brothers and she walked away with them.

They walked and they walked and soon they came to a strange village with rows of houses. They took her to the centre of the village where the chief's house was. She realized now that they had not taken her to *Damelahamid*. When she looked at the strange village she finally realized that the people she was with were not her brothers at all, but two different types. At first, when they met her, they had had the appearance of her brothers. She knew now that something was wrong.

They stood outside the door and a voice came from inside, "Have you accomplished your mission? Have you got what you were looking for?" And they answered, "Yes, we have. She is with us, here now." And the voice said, "Enter, then. Bring her in that I may examine her."

They entered the house. At the head sat a big chief. He was a *huge* person and she noticed that there was something different about him. Although he was a person, there was a marked distinction about him. He had the appearance of an old man who had just woken up from a deep sleep, with sleep still showing in his eyes. He said, "Fine. You have done well. Bring her and seat her beside me. She is going to become my bride."

And the princess cried. She cried all night. She did not sleep. She cried. She knew now that she had been abducted by strange people. Suddenly she felt something tickling her bottom. She looked down to see what it was. There was a little field mouse or *taboggan*. She followed him to a little house. A voice came from inside, "Come in, *hlicht*, if you are the person who has been abducted by bears." She entered. She knew now that it was the bear people who had abducted her. There was a fire in the centre of the house and at the other end sat a little old lady. She said, "*Hlicht*, would you rip off some of the frills from your *delhz*. Throw them in the fire for me, will you, *hlicht*?" So she did. She pulled off some of the frills from her *delhz* and threw them into the fire.

The little old lady very quickly pulled them out of the fire and piled the wool in front of her. She was very happy. This was all the payment that she had asked for. She said, "All right. I will tell you what has happened. You have been abducted by the bear people because you criticized the *chehū* that was on the path that you slipped on. It was their chief's deposit — the one you have been brought to. From now on, they plan to keep you and they are going to test you. They are trying to find out why you feel so superior. They are going to compare your *chehū* with their. This is what I want you to do. Tomorrow they are going to ask you to go and get some wood and there will be some children with you. It is their job to bring wood for the household.

"When you go out with them, collect all wet wood. Do not pick up any dry wood. And when you want to *yon nelhz tle lo guenkū dum tsewen*, dig a hole in the ground deep enough so that it can be covered up and there will be no odour. Drop your *chehū* in there, cover it up and take a couple of your bracelets and leave them on top. The youngsters will observe you. They won't look at you too closely. But don't worry about them. Just do what I ask you."

The old lady continued, "After you have gained these people's confidence, one day find a heavy piece of wood and tie it tightly to the children. It will take two or three days. Then head downstream. Just follow the stream. When you come to the ocean, you will find a man there, in his boat. Call him right away. His name is *Gudeloch*. Call him right away and with your first statement tell him that you are going to marry him. Ask him to come and pick you up in his boat. This man, *Gudeloch*, is a *nochnoch* and he will help you. Now do as I tell you and I will be there to help you."

The princess left. She went back to her house. She was happy now. She knew what she had to do. She had been helped by a little *owenzeets*. The next day she got up quite early and all the men of the village had gone off to hunt. She forgot that she had to find wet wood. She was used to dry wood being used in her own village. She gathered a bundle of dry wood and tied it to the children. She had to defecate so she picked a good spot. She made sure that the children watched her. While they weren't looking, she dug a hole in the ground and left her deposit and covered it up. She then took off two of her bracelets and left them on the top.

Then she went back to the village with the children. They had a lot of wood and made a big fire. The hunters were back, soaked and wet. They took off their blankets and shook them on the fire and the fire went out. The wood was too dry. The men took her wood and threw it out and got some fresh wood themselves. She remembered then that she had to use wet wood. Then they heard the chanting of little children outside, "Grandpa, grandpa, look at what we have got! We have found the *chehū* of your adversary. Look at what it is like! We have it with us!"

The big chief said, "Bring it in. I want to inspect it." They brought in the two bracelets and gave them to him and he inspected them. "It is justified. This young lady is justified in criticizing my *chehū*. If I had wastes like this, I would be in a position to criticize other people also."

They were happy with her now. The next day she went out and got the right kind of wood and the whole village was very pleased with her.

Finally, the day came when she went out to where she had marked some really wet wood. She tied it together and then tied it to the children. They could barely move, their load was so heavy. And then she ran. She ran downstream. She soon came to the shore of the ocean. And, true to the prediction, there was a canoe out in the middle and a man was sitting in the canoe. She shouted *"Gudeloch*, come and get me. I will marry you. Please come and get me." *Gudeloch* picked up a little stick that he carried and hit the stern of his canoe. The canoe was propelled by itself and it landed right on the shore where the girl was.

Gudeloch said, "Get into the canoe and we will get away from here." She got into the canoe just as a whole army of bears, black bears, brown bears, grizzly bears, came. *Gudeloch* pushed the canoe out into the water and waited for them. The bears thought that they would be able to pull the princess back on shore. *Gudeloch*, however, was a *nochnoch* and he stood on the shore and slew many of the bears. He was waiting for the big bear. With a growling and a thundering noise, the big bear appeared. A big grizzly bear appeared, really very frightening. The bear intended to pull *Gudeloch* down quickly but *Gudeloch* didn't allow that to happen. He did not kill the big grizzly but took his little stick, hit the stern of his canoe and off he and the princess went. They left the big bear behind.

It wasn't long until he came to his own home on the shore of the ocean. When they arrived they were greeted by another woman, apparently *Gudeloch*'s wife. She was very happy to see that *Gudeloch* had brought another woman. She said to him, "You are very thoughtful. You have brought me a sister at last. I am very happy to have a sister. I haven't got a sister of my own. I am so very happy that you have brought me a sister." She immediately called her "sister" and invited her into the house, chattering all the time.

Gudeloch cautioned her, saying, "Go about your business and let the lady rest." So she did. She prepared the dinner and they had a big meal. She herself did not eat. The young princess noticed this; *Gudeloch*'s wife did not eat with them but she had prepared a real feast for herself and *Gudeloch*. Late at night, when it was time to go to bed, they told her where to sleep. She had her own *tyak tyak* or room and *Gudeloch*'s wife had her own *tyak tyak* on the other side of this room. *Gudeloch* himself had his own sleeping place.

Gudeloch, however, took his canoe and went out to hunt because he found hunting much better at night. The young princess was sleeping when she was wakened by a very frightening noise. She did not know what the noise was. It sounded like, "Shrrrk, shrrrk, shrrk, shrrrrrk!" She was very frightened and she thought of going to see if *Gudeloch*'s wife could do anything to help her. But when she went out of her room she found that it was *Gudeloch*'s wife who was making the noise. She was eating the seals that *Gudeloch* had brought home. The princess had noticed that *Gudeloch*'s wife had not prepared the seals for their evening meal. She had cooked something quite different. She was eating the seals raw and ate a whole seal at a time.

The princess noticed a very strange thing. *Gudeloch*'s wife was a wolverine. She recognized her as both *Gudeloch*'s wife and a wolverine at the same time. She was a *nochnoch*. *Gude-*

loch was also a *nochnoch*, and therefore anything could happen. They were both capable of doing anything.

When the princess saw *Gudeloch*'s wife eating, she remembered what the little *owenzeets* had told her. She had told her that *Gudeloch* had a *nochnoch* for a wife and said that she should not do anything to offend her. So she very quickly returned to her bed, covered herself up and pretended to be asleep. But *Gudeloch*'s wife, *We tsim nossik*, felt that someone was watching her and she choked herself into a paralytic fit. When she regained consciousness, she entered the princess's bedroom, took the girl and killed her by pulling her heart out of her breast. She took her outside and threw her down on the hillside.

The next morning, when *Gudeloch* returned from his hunting, he found the princess and realized what had happened to her. Being a *nochnoch* himself, he took the girl and replaced her heart in her breast, covered it up and brought her back to life. She woke up as if she had been in a deep dream, and *Gudeloch* told her "We are going to return to my house and I caution you, whatever you do, don't pay any attention to what you hear." He added "She won't harm you. She is not really angry with you. She is angry because she choked on her food. So if it happens again, don't be frightened. Don't do anything."

Gudeloch took her back in to the house. His wife was there and she said, "Oh, *Gudeloch*, you have brought my sister back. How nice of you. I have missed her. I didn't know where she went. She just went out for a little while."

Gudeloch did not say anything. He just attacked his wife, killed her and threw her out of the house. But it wasn't long after this that *We tsim nossik* came dancing back into the house, saying, "Oh, I went for a little walk. I had a nice little walk, and I am glad that you are all very well in this house." Because she was a *nochnoch*, she could really only be killed by a very special method. *Gudeloch* knew this but he was not prepared to kill her at this time. He was just punishing her by attacking her and killing her temporarily and throwing her out

89

of the house. *We tsim nossik* knew this. *Gudeloch* was just showing her that he was particularly angry over what had happened.

During that day, the young princess was quite pleased with her surroundings. She felt comfortable in the presence of *Gudeloch*, and *Gudeloch*'s wife was so kind to her that she forgot her experiences of the night before. At night *Gudeloch* left to hunt more seals and the two women went to bed.

The princess fell asleep, but deep in her sleep she heard the noise again. Because of her past experience with the bears, she became very frightened. Before she realized what she was doing, she had jumped out of bed to see what was happening. And there she was again! *Gudeloch*'s wife was eating seals again, and again she became upset and choked on her food. The princess very quickly returned to her bed and covered herself up. But when *Gudeloch*'s wife regained consciousness, she went into the princess's bedroom and took her, tore her heart out, mutilated her and tossed her down the hillside.

When *Gudeloch* returned the next morning, he knew that his wife had to be punished. He said nothing, left the princess lying outside, went into the house and saw his wife. *We tsim nossik* was running about getting things done. She said to *Gudeloch*, "I don't know where my sister is. She must have got up early and gone into the woods for a walk." But *Gudeloch* did not pay any attention. He just said, "Oh, be quiet! Bring in the seals and start preparing some breakfast for me. I am very hungry." *We tsim nossik* started to prepare meat for *Gudeloch*. *Gudeloch* picked up a spear or *daptlhz*, and began putting on a new spear-head. It was very sharp. Every time that *We tsim nossik* went past, she turned to him and said, "Oh, *Gudeloch*, I have a feeling that you have evil thoughts when you are doing that. I have a feeling that you intend to kill me."

Gudeloch did not pay any attention to her. When he had finished preparing his *daptlhz*, he suddenly attacked *We tsim nossik*, stabbed her in the neck and threw her into the fire. He then chopped off her head, which he kept, and threw her body out of the house. He then brought in the young princess from outside. He laid her badly mutilated body down and washed all the sand from her heart, then replaced it in her body. He then took *We tsim nossik*'s head, walked around it four times, and the young girl came back to life just as if she had been in a deep dream.

Gudeloch said to her, "*We tsim nossik* is not really angry with you. She is only angry because you startled her and she choked on her food. You must be very careful when you hear a noise at night not to pay any attention to it. You need never fear the bears again. We are situated in such a place that they will never come after you." *Gudeloch* prepared some food and after they had eaten *We tsim nossik* came in, dancing and smiling. "I see you have just finished eating. I am so happy for you both. You enjoy life so much. It was so nice out that I decided to go into the bush and have a little sleep." *Gudeloch* did not pay any attention to her. He just went about the day's business, and in the evening prepared to go out again. His last instructions to the young princess were, "Whatever happens, don't stare. Just allow everything to go on. Don't be afraid, because nothing will harm you. She has no intention of harming you as long as you don't startle her."

When the little princess went to bed she was so worried she couldn't sleep. She felt a little tickle on her bottom again, and she saw the tiny *owenzeets*. She followed it to a little house where a voice called out for her to enter. She pulled pieces of wool from her belt to pay the *owenzeets*, and she was told, "You have gone through your ordeal because of lapses of memory. *Gudeloch*'s wife does not wish to harm you, but she gets quite angry when she chokes on her food. You have learned your lesson the hard way. However, there are more trials ahead of you.

"*Gudeloch* himself will put you through a trial. He likes you very much and he wants to marry you, but you have to pass a test. When he returns tomorrow, he is going to tell you that he has been infested with bugs. His hair will be full of bugs. He will ask you to clean it for him, and when you are doing this, you will find all sorts of monsters appearing. Although they appear frightful, don't be afraid of them. I will help you.

"Here are some little sticks. Hold them in your hand so no one will see them. You must pretend to take the bugs from his hair and put them in your mouth. While you are doing this, break off a little piece of stick and spit it into the fire. *Gudeloch* will think that you are destroying the bugs. They are really imaginary bugs and you don't have to be afraid of them. *Gudeloch* wants to find out if you are afraid of him or not."

The little princess took the sticks and went back to her bed and slept. When the noise woke her, she just covered her head and didn't move. The next morning, she heard *Gudeloch* and his wife talking down on the shore. They were packing all the seals that he had killed during the night. *Gudeloch* carried two at a time as if they were feathers. Then they all had breakfast.

After they had eaten, *Gudeloch* said to the little princess, "I have been having problems with my hair. It is infested with bugs. I would be very thankful if you would clean it for me."

The young girl remembered what the *owenzeets* had told her and asked *Gudeloch* to lie down on the floor beside her and put his head on her lap. As she started to part his hair, she suddenly saw thousands of frightening bugs, all shapes and types. She just managed to overcome her fear. She picked up her little sticks and started to work. To her surprise, the minute she touched one of the bugs, it disappeared. However, she put the stick in her mouth, broke off a piece which made a cracking sound, and spit the piece into the fire. The fire flared up. She continued until all the bugs had disappeared from one side of *Gudeloch's* head. Then she said, "Would you please turn over now so that I can do the other side?"

The other side was more frightening than the first. It appeared as if the bugs were going to attack her. However, she overcame her fear and cleaned the hair on this side the same way that she had the other. When all the monsters had disappeared, she told *Gudeloch* that she had thoroughly cleaned his hair.

Gudeloch was very pleased that she had passed this test. He said to her, "All these years I have been looking for a human for a wife. I never found anyone whom I wanted to keep. But you have passed the test and I have decided that you will become my human wife. Tonight, when I leave, there will be the noise again and you must deliberately interrupt my wife and let her do exactly as she did before. She will kill you and throw your body out. But this time I am going to destroy her once and for all. I know how to do it."

That evening, he again left to hunt seals. The little princess heard the noise again after she had gone to bed. "Shrrk, shrrrk, shrrrk!" When *We tsim nossik* saw that she was being watched, she choked on a raw seal and fell backwards. When she regained her strength, she attacked the little princess, pulled her heart from her body and threw her on the hillside.

When *Gudeloch* returned, he saw what had happened. When he entered the house, his wife was happy to see him and said, "Oh I am glad to see you back. Your breakfast is ready. Unfortunately, my sister has gone for a walk in the bush. I haven't seen her since." *Gudeloch* did not pay any attention to her. He sat down and prepared his *daptlhz*. His wife said, "I think you have an evil thought in your head. You are going to kill me." He replied, "Be quiet and go about your business." When *Gudeloch* was ready, he attacked his wife and stabbed her in the back of her neck with the *daptlhz* and held her in the fire until she stopped struggling.

He then methodically dissected his wife who turned out to be a wolverine. He washed every piece of the body in a prepared bath of *melhuish* or roots used for decontamination. This was to combat any extraordinary strength that the *nochnoch* might use to return to life. *Gudeloch* then picked up the young princess from the hillside, brought her back in the house, lay her down and washed her body. He put her heart back in her breast, walked around her four times with *We tsim nossik*'s head, and she came back to life.

Gudeloch showed the princess what had happened. "I have

destroyed her permanently now. She will never come back to haunt you or torment you. I will get rid of her and you will become my wife." He took the pieces of *We tsim nossik*'s body out in his canoe and dropped them at different places in the ocean, to remain there forever. He came back and took the young princess as his wife.

Analogues

A common Tsimshian story tells of animals assuming the shape of males and marrying young girls. After giving birth to children, the girls are returned to their homes with their offspring. Boas states that these stories are essentially characteristic of the Tlingit and the Tsimshian, and the Haida is influenced by either of these.[1] It is also part of Bella Coola and Rivers Inlet tradition. Boas finds the story divided into four parts: 1. The girl taken away by the bear whom she scolded; 2. The marriage of the girl with the lake-being; 3. The woman carried away by the Killer Whales; 4. The origin of the crests of the Raven clan. He records ten versions of the Girl Who is Taken by the Bear[2] — either a Black Bear or a Grizzly. One difference in Ken Harris's story is that the girl has two brothers (bears who assume sibling personalities) who appear to help her. The Tlingit, Bella Coola and Rivers Inlet tales introduce only one man. In one Tsimshian version, the girl is asked to sacrifice her ear-ornaments before the Mouse Woman will help her. In another, it is a woman who is half rock who gives her advice. In a Haida version, Pitch Woman assists.

In his Haida version Swanton also describes "a woman who was half rock" sitting in the corner of the house as the helpful accomplice.[3] All versions use copper bracelets to represent the girl's excrement.

The various stories continue differently. In "The Story of Part

---

[1] Boas, *Tsimshian Mythology*, p. 748.
[2] Ibid., p. 836.
[3] Swanton, *Haida Texts*, p. 336.

Summer"[4] the girl marries a Black-Bear Chief, and she is later rescued by her four real brothers and two dogs, Red and Spots, who all help to kill the Black Bears. This girl gives birth to two boys who live with their mother in her own village for a few years before returning to the Bear people. Boas should be consulted for the many other adventures experienced by the girl.[5] Most of them involve the girl's escape from the Bears and subsequent marriage to either a bird or a sea anemone or to a son of the Sun. She gives birth to a son after the original wife, usually a wolverine, is killed. Tsimshian, Stikine, and Haida versions mention a delousing scene just as the girl is rescued from the Bears, therefore earlier than in the Harris tale.

Swanton also takes frogs out of the girl's rescuer's hair.[6] His name is Sagadila. Swanton's story ends with the adventures of the girl's son and includes the white sea otter fur incident, the Killer Whale kidnapping scene, and the rescue, with the subsequent disappearance from the fifth of a nest of five boxes, of the mother on their return to Q!adō. Swanton collected the whole story in Masset as well as Skidegate, and found that in all of the Haida versions, the adventures with the Killer Whale occupied a disproportionately large space.

---

[4] Boas, *Tsimshian Mythology*, p. 279.
[5] Ibid., pp. 839-45.
[6] Swanton, *Haida Texts*, p. 336.

2.

Gooch nach no emgit Finds a Bride

This story points out that no one, or nothing, should be overlooked, no matter how small. The little chipmunk demonstrates this in the song he sings at the presentation feast.

The word "space" is used instead of "sky" because the latter is too limiting.

Soon after the young princess and *Gudeloch* were married, she became pregnant. A boy was born. *Gudeloch* was very pleased but he knew, being a *nochnoch*, what lay in the future. When it came time for the naming of the baby, he sent invitations to the ends of the earth. He invited every moving creature. He invited the people, the animals, everything. They all came to the feast that *Gudeloch* prepared for his son.

Gudeloch made the presentation at the feast. Because he had invited the whole world, he decided to call his son *Gooch nach no emgit*, meaning "he is known throughout the world." He was known by the fishes in the ocean, known by the birds in the sky, known by every form of life on land.

Each animal, on making his presentation to *Gudeloch*'s son, promised that he would help him in one form or another. Each one did his dance and made his presentation, down to the smallest animal that lived on earth. The last person to dance and sing his song was the little chipmunk:

"My blanket may be of patched pattern,
    But I am just as important as the rest of your guests."
He had something to offer the baby, too.

After the naming-feast, *Gudeloch* took his son everywhere with him. They hunted. *Gudeloch* taught him how to use his self-propelled canoe, the canoe that travelled in any direction. *Gudeloch* taught his son thoroughly. And, being the son of a *nochnoch*, he became in many ways a *nochnoch* himself. There were things that humans couldn't do which he was able to do.

He grew up and his father decided that it was time for his son and his wife to return to their village in *Damelahamid*. He filled up his canoe with food and goods and then showed them which way to go.

So *Gooch nach no emgit* and his mother returned. They went up the river and they came to *Damelahamid*. Everyone in the village was amazed. They were seen coming and word spread to the chief that a very strange canoe was coming up the river. It was self-powered. It contained only a young man and a woman and they seemed to recognize the woman as the long-lost princess of *Damelahamid*. This was all the chief needed to hear. He wanted to believe, so he went down himself to meet the canoe. When the canoe approached the shores of *Damela-hamid* he recognized his daughter and he was very happy. When the canoe landed, he called her by name. She answered, "My father, I have been away for a long time. I am married and now it is time for me to come back. I am bringing my son. My husband cannot come, because he can never be with us. It was never destined for him to be with us. He is a *nochnoch*, but his son has come with me and he will be a part of our family. His name is *Gooch nach no emgit*." The people of *Damelaha-mid* were very happy with the return of the princess with her son, a new grandson of the House.

Life went on normally in the city of *Damelahamid*. The son was very happy. He enjoyed having grandparents and cousins and friends. One day, he remembered that his father had told him that somewhere, out in space, was a daughter of the sun, a very beautiful girl. She had hair just like gold, that fell right down to her ankles. He decided he was going to visit her. He wanted to take her for his wife.

He discussed his idea with his mother, but she said, "No, I don't think you should go. I know your father has discussed this girl frequently, but it is a very hazardous journey and I don't think you should attempt it, not only for yourself but also for the sake of your companions."

Gooch nach no emgit always had several people who travelled everywhere with him. He answered his mother, "No, I do not think I will need any of my companions. I think I know exactly how I am going to make the journey." And, one day, he set off in his canoe until he came to the appointed take-off point. He stood there and sang a very beautiful chant:

"I know, I know that on the other side of this great
big space lives a very beautiful girl. I have heard so
much about her. I am going to journey to that far
away place just to see her."

He pulled a strand of his long hair from his head and another and tied them together. The hair came alive and pointed directly to the moon. The beautiful girl was a daughter of the sun and lived on the moon. *Gooch nach no emgit's* canoe started to move along the path indicated by the mysterious strands of hair and he went on singing, chanting his song. He pulled many more strands of hair from his head and tied them end to end until, finally, he came to a door which was closed.

He stood outside this door and sang, "I have finally made the journey. I have come to your door but it is closed and I cannot get in." While he was singing, the door opened and on the other side he saw a very beautiful girl sitting at the head of the house.

She was alone. Her hair, just as his father had described it, covered her shoulders and hung down to her ankles. It was like gold. *Gooch nach no emgit* walked through the doorway. The girl looked at him and smiled and put her hand out. *Gooch nach no emgit* took her hand and said, "I have come a long way to see you. I want you to be my bride." The girl consented. She said, "I knew you were coming. I have waited many years for you to come." He picked her up and carried her out of the house and into his canoe. They returned by the path he had made from the strands of his hair.

They arrived on the shores of *Damelahamid* and went to *Gooch nach no emgit*'s house where he showed his new bride to his grandfather and his mother. They were all very happy. Everyone on earth envied *Gooch nach no emgit*. They all knew that he had a very special wife.

Analogues

In a Tlingit version quoted by Boas the boy is not born until after the mother returned to her father's house.[1] Therefore, he has to visit his father who then gives him his gifts; abalone shells, sharks' teeth, and a magic club for killing animals. A Tsimshian version has his mother giving him an otter club, bow, and arrows. His mother is the one who gives a potlatch and names her son. In both a Haida version from Skidegate and a Tsimshian version, the hero elopes with his uncle's daughter.

[1] Boas, *Tsimshian Mythology*, p. 840.

3.

The Kidnapping

Windottha was a medicine that all warriors and hunters carried in a little bag on their belts. It came from the new growth on the top of the poplars. It was mixed into a very hard paste like chewing gum and stuck in the mouth behind the teeth. The medicine gave energy. One mouthful of *windottha* enabled a person to keep going all day.

The House of *Hagbegwatku* from which *Gooch nach no emgit* came adopted the killer whale as one of their clan crests. They made the "meeting of the whales" for a door entrance and the design appeared on their blankets as well. The "meeting" refers to the defeated whales returning to their home in the ocean coming upon the slower whales who were still in pursuit, and telling them that all was lost. Ken Harris's own blanket that he used when he was *Nagwa* had six whales, three on each side. He points out that the blanket is also seen among the Tsimshians and the Haidas.

A second totem pole was also erected outside the House of *Hagbegwatku*. This was the first pole erected after the *gilhast*. It had a white killer whale with a woman riding on its back. The killer whale pole is also found in Alaska with the Tlingits on Shakes Island, where *Weeshakes* is the chief. These people have always been associated with Ken Harris's people's history.

Ken Harris speaks of the importance of this crest: "Although our relatives among the Tsimshians, Haidas, Kwakiutls, Tlingits, and Nishgas are allowed to use some parts of the killer whale to show that they belong to the House of *Hagbegwatku*, there is *no* other House of the Killer Whale clan allowed to show the *white* killer whale. I, as *Hagbegwatku*, am the only person allowed to have it. When I was a baby I was elevated to the ranks of a prince of *Damelahamid*. I received the title of *Deelepzeb*. My father had a white killer whale made and he called a feast at which all the chiefs gathered. He carried me on one arm and the white killer whale in the other as I went through the ritual elevating me to the station of a prince. I have this killer whale in my possession today."

Life was back to normal in *Damelahamid*. *Gooch nach no emgit* became one of the greatest providers of food for the city. Because his canoe was self-propelled, it did not require much manpower but he always had companions with him to help him in everything he did. He hunted daily, always getting enough for his own household and distributing the rest to the people.

One day while he was hunting he saw a beautiful white-furred animal. He looked at it closely and saw that it was an albino sea-otter or *mess plong*. He killed it. He took it home to his wife and told her, "This is going to be your own." There was a little blood on the white fur so she took it down to the ocean to clean it. The fur was very beautiful. It could be rubbed in any direction. She carried it out to a large rock, stepping on stones in the water, and started washing the blood from the *mess plong*. Suddenly she had a very strange feeling that she was moving. She looked up and found that she was actually on the back of a great big white killer whale. A fin appeared and she took hold of it. She hung on with her right hand, still holding the fur in her left. She shouted for help, and the children who were playing on the shore saw her. They went to get *Gooch nach no emgit*. He saw his wife standing on the back of the big white killer whale. He recognized the whale as *Goesmessnech*.

He knew exactly what he had to do. His father had told him of several things that would happen and what he could do about them. He called for volunteers in the village and from them he selected only those whom he could trust and who had been purified. *Gooch nach no emgit*, being a *nochnoch* himself could recognize those who had the highest degree of purification.

He led them all to his canoe, and his mother pulled out the big box which his father had given to them. It had a special rope in it. It was called an *olhunku*. *Gooch nach no emgit* put the box in his canoe and they all went in pursuit of *Goesmessnech*. They came to *An twe lilbergue*, the spot where *Gooch nach no emgit* had to go down to the bottom of the ocean to find his wife. He told his companions, "I cannot take you any further. I know what I have to do. I will still need you." He gave them strict instructions to keep themselves in a state of highest purification while he was gone. He threw the *olhunku* over the side of the canoe and as it dropped to the bottom of the ocean it left an opening like a shaft. *Gooch nach no emgit* slipped down the opening and found land at the bottom. There was no water around. It seemed quite normal.

He ran into many animals, animals which his father had introduced him to. They said, "*Gooch nach no emgit*, we knew you were coming and we will help you. *Goesmessnech* went that way with your wife." They pointed out the direction.

Gooch nach no emgit set out right away. He put some *windottha* in his mouth. All the animals he met pointed in the direction *Goesmessnech* had taken. They all offered help and he gave each of them some *windottha*. Finally he came to a city. It seemed very well established; in fact, exactly like *Damelaha-mid*. He saw the chief's house in the centre. He went up to it cautiously and looked through a knot-hole in the wall. He saw his wife seated at the head of the house with *Goesmessnech*.

Goesmessnech was giving orders to his servant to get some wood, an especial type of wood for a fire for his new wife. The servant's name was *Gid tse tgan*. He took an axe or *helz le gyawku* when he went out.

Gooch nach no emgit followed him. They came to a big tree which was hollow. He slipped inside the tree when *Gid tse tgan* was not looking. When the servant tried to chop down the tree with his *helz le gyawku*, *Gooch nach no emgit* took a bite out of the axe. When the servant saw this, he sat down and wept. He spoke to himself "I am very sad because I have destroyed my master's favourite *helz le gyawku*."

Gooch nach no emgit went up to him and asked him why he was so sad. He replied, "I have broken this *helz le gyawku* which belongs to my master and I fear his anger." *Gooch nach no emgit* said, "I think I can fix it for you." He turned around, put it up to his mouth and returned the broken parts that he had bitten off. It was just like new when he had finished. He returned it to the servant who was very happy.

Gid tse tgan said, "I know who you are now and I will help you regain your wife. I am getting wood for a fire. The rocks for heating the fire are nearly ready now as they are getting hot. When I return with this load of wood, I will be asked to get some water."

While they were talking they heard a woman singing, coming their way. *Gid tse tgan* said, "Hide inside the tree! It is my wife. She has come to help gather the wood." His wife came and started to sniff around. She said, "Hmmm. I am sure I smell *Gooch nach no emgit*." Her husband told her "Don't be silly. How do you expect *Gooch nach no emgit* to come here? He is a human. He hasn't got any extraordinary power. Pick up your load and take it home. They will be waiting for us. And when you get there, don't talk foolishly. No one is going to listen to you anyway."

She took her wood and went back. The two men made their plan. The servant said, "When I go and get the water, I will have deposited you inside the house in one of these logs. When I return with it, I will stumble and throw the water on the red-hot stones. It will create a lot of steam in the house. You must pick up your wife and get out as fast as you can, because I am going to swell and block the doorway."

So it happened. *Gooch nach no emgit* was inside the log and he could see his wife sitting at the head of the house. *Gid tse tgan* went out with two large *thwel-lahz*, or bags made of cedar bark, to get the water. When he returned, he fell at the entrance and threw the water on the big red-hot stones.

A fog of steam rose up. *Gooch nach no emgit* jumped out of his log, picked up his wife and ran out of the house, jumping over *Gid tse tgan* who was swelling in size. He quickly became so big he blocked the door. *Gid tse tgan* used to swell every time he fell. His wife was really a little bird and she had to pick away at his stomach in order to get the swelling down. She picked away, picked away, picked away. It took a long time for the swelling to reduce. Some of the faster killer whales managed to get through the door, including *Goesmessnech*, and started after *Gooch nach no emgit* and his wife.

They ran back to where the rope was. All the animals who had promised to help did. They helped to slow down the chase. *Gooch nach no emgit* pulled on the rope and his companions on the top of the ocean pulled them back up. They climbed into the canoe and headed back to *Damelahamid*.

They pulled the canoe right into their house and they blocked all the doors. They reinforced the house with pitch. Soon the killer whales came in pursuit and the water rose to cover the house. The whales rammed the house many times but could not manage to break in. Finally, they gave up and turned around and left. The water returned to normal. *Gooch nach no emgit* had defeated *Goesmessnech*, the large white killer whale.

Analogues

Boas tells of many different adventures the youth has on his way to the House of the Killer Whales.[1] The Kwakiutl tribes also have versions of this part of the story. Encounters are with a Heron, Blind Geese, an old woman. Tsimshian versions also include a Beaver, a Clam, a Codfish, and a Halibut. In a Haida tale the hero meets a Mouse. In a Tlingit story he meets pale people, whom he paints red, also Halibut people. Tobacco is very often the bribe with which the various people met are propitiated.

Boas mentions twenty versions of the wood-splitting incident, included in Tsimshian, Tlingit, Haida, Nass, Seshelt, and Kwakiutl stories. The wood-chopping slaves number from one to three. In one Nass version, the woman herself is to be cooked and eaten. In all versions, the man escapes with his wife.

[1] Boas, *Tsimshian Mythology*, p. 842.

THE ORIGIN OF
WEEGET AND *QUISKEN*

This shows the symbiosis of existence between the natural world and that of the supernatural. Human beings able to travel to Heaven may not return to earth, but their offspring can make this journey. This keeps the supernatural origin of the people of *Damelahamid* alive in their minds.

1.

Strange Journeys

The word *quisken* means pitch. Ken Harris points out that the pitch from a spruce tree is different from that of other trees. When chewed, it turns pink, and when burned, it runs like syrup. At this time, Ken Harris's uncle, Stanley Williams, is called *Quisken*. He is a chief next to the Head Chief at Kitwanga.

Bertie Russell, of Kitsegucla, is called *Weeget*, and he is another chief of very high rank. The only occasion on which *Weeget* or *Trēnsem* took the form of a raven was when he was very hungry and stole whalemeat from Indians who were dressing it on the beach. The following is Ken Harris's version of the story:

"*Trēnsem* tried to approach the people on the beach, but they were aware that he was in the vicinity and had set up guards and barricades around the beached whale. They would not allow him near. He was very hungry and did not know what to do. He saw a little raven and he killed it and took the skin and wore it. He was very cautious at first. He managed to get close to the whale by using several funny manoeuvres such as walking in an erratic pattern until he was able to get close enough to peck the whale meat. Soon the people paid no attention to him. When he had eaten his fill, he became very confident, and he flew into the large hole at the rectal end of the whale. The people watched him dive into the rectum and fly through the whale and out of the front end. They heard him say something. He sat on a little branch and said, "*Tsim golhz welhzbone!*" Translated this means, "The rear end of the whale!" He dived through the whale again and emerged out of the front end. The children laughed and one of the oldest heard what he was saying. He told the older people to listen. *Trēnsem* repeated it and dived through the whale again. The older people said, "Oh! It's *Trēnsem!*" and grabbed sticks and stones and chased him. He got away by a narrow escape."

Trēnsem is known all over Canada. He was always a trickster. *Trēnsem*, who has a supernatural origin, is still around today. He cannot return to Heaven until "the end of time." Ken Harris says that his importance lies in the fact that he is supernatural because he was born in Heaven and he acts as a constant reminder to the people of *Damelahamid* that they also originated in Heaven.

Another interesting sidelight is that the Northern Woodpecker has a black tail which is supposed to have come when it was unable to fly cleanly through the *mismah*.

In the time of *Damelahamid* a chief took a wife of whom he was very fond. She was a young woman and she soon became pregnant. At the time when she was ready to have her baby, she became ill and died. Her husband did not wish to cremate her as was the usual fashion. So he ordered a house to be built, not too far away from his own house. It was also very close to an archery range. He put his wife's remains inside the house and closed it up. He used to visit her frequently.

Young warriors used to practise on the archery range. After they had shot at the targets, they would go and check the targets and pick up their arrows. One day, before they had a chance to pick up their arrows, a little naked boy came running out of the house, picked up all the arrows and ran back into the house. They shot a few more and the same thing happened. They could not catch the little boy as he was too fast, and it was taboo for them to go inside the house. They went back to the village and told the chief what had happened.

Everyone thought about this. They decided the little boy would have to be captured. They dug trenches in front of the house and covered them over with camouflage. Some of the warriors hid in the trenches.

They started archery practice, and, after all the arrows had been shot, the little boy came running out to collect them. The hidden people jumped out of the trenches and guarded the entrance of the house. The warriors who had been shooting the arrows chased after the little boy and he ran to his house but found that other people had blocked his path.

He stopped and was captured. They wrapped him in a

blanket and took him back to the chief. The wise men had decided that the chief's wife must have had her baby after she had died and the baby had lived in the house until he was old enough to run around. He had been attracted by the arrows.

He did not put up any resistance but he did not want to eat. They tried everything. He continued to grow, but he did not eat. There was one thing that he kept repeating, *"Adelhz leeai. Adelhz leeai."* The chief asked all the wise men what he was saying. No one knew. They made many baskets, because that was what it sounded like, and gave them to him but he just threw them away.

They then discovered that at the edge of the village there lived an old man who was said to be very wise. The chief sent for him and said, "I want you to listen to my son and see if you can understand what he wants."

The old man listened and then said, "Oh, it is a very simple thing. At the end of the village is a waterfall and right beside it is a big spruce tree. He wants the pitch from the tree. I suggest you take him out to this big spruce tree, set it on fire and we will see what he does."

They did. They took the little boy out to the tree and set fire to it. The pitch started to run. The little boy quickly went over and stood underneath the tree, allowing the pitch to run over his body until it was completely covered. Then he ran underneath the nearby waterfall. The pitch solidified and his skin peeled off and fell at his feet. The boy walked away from his piled-up skin. He now looked entirely different. He had the appearance of a *nochnoch* or a divine person.

They took him back to his house. He could eat now. He ate everything that everyone else did. He started to develop and he became very fond of his little cousin. They became inseparable.

One day, when they were both in their late teens, the young man told his cousin, "Today, we are going after something special. I know that at the end of the world we can gain entrance into heaven. However, we need transportation to get there."

They had to go beyond the *mismah* or through a hole in space. They needed special transportation. They came across a pileated woodpecker, pecking away at a tree. They took a blunt-end arrow and with one shot they killed it and then skinned it. The young man put the skin in his *eez* or pocket. A little further on, they found a northern woodpecker and they killed and skinned it, too. The young man gave this skin to his cousin. And they went where no one could see them.

The young man said, "I want you to watch me carefully." He put the bird's skin on his head and, through some very strange action, he shrank into the skin which completely covered him. Now he could fly. When he returned he removed his bird's skin and asked his cousin to do the same thing. After some persuasion, his cousin did the same thing and found that he could fly too. They both flew around. They said nothing of all this when they returned to the village. They practised flying every day. Finally, they were ready to leave. Only at certain times of the year could you pass through the *mismah*. They took some *windottha* with them. This drug would prevent them from being frightened of anything and it would also nourish them. They told the chief that they were leaving.

They began to fly. They were on the way to the *mismah* through which they had to fly to reach Heaven. As they flew over the village, the people looked up and shouted, "You, who was born from a dead mother, do you think you can gain entrance into Heaven by going through the *mismah?*" They flew over the village and answered, "*Tsuni, tsuni, tsuni, tsuni.* Oh yes. Oh yes. Oh, yes. Oh, yes."

They kept flying until they got to the *mismah*. They could hear it and they finally saw it. It was a fiery opening that opened three times quickly and on the fourth stayed open a little longer. They watched it. On the fourth opening they flew through the *mismah*. The pileated woodpecker flew through with no problem, but the northern woodpecker's tail got burnt. They landed on the other side. They were now in Heaven.

The Chief-in-Heaven was called *Simoigetdamla ha*, and he

had two daughters. The younger one was called *Tsim ohl*. The two men made a wish that the chief's two daughters would go and get their own water, even though servants usually did this for them. That morning, the eldest daughter woke up and said, "Let us go outside and get some water." They went to the pond and saw two beautiful birds. They had never seen them before and they were anxious to capture them. The older daughter asked *Tsim ohl* if she had anything they could use. "Yes, I have got something that looks like a string." They made a snare and set it in the path that the birds seemed to use. They soon trapped them, but when they picked them up the birds just dropped dead. The girls were very unhappy, but they decided to keep the birds. The oldest one kept the *ha-ut* and the youngest the *gidwinthu*. They took them home.

After they had gone to bed that night, they woke up in the middle of the night and found two young men sleeping with them. A princess was guarded well in her sleeping quarters. Her suitors had a kind of competition. The one who got past the guards and managed to sleep the night with the girl became her husband. That was the extent of the wedding ceremony.

In the morning the chief knew that his two daughters had had men with them. He had been expecting this. He told his daughters to bring their young men to breakfast. When he saw them, he knew that they were not ordinary people. They were not people of Heaven and he knew it would take a very special type of person to come through the *mismah*. He agreed to the double union. Soon, both girls became pregnant.

They had sons, both being born about the same time. The chief took the little boys and bathed them. Each time he did this, the boys would stretch and in a short time they both became very tall. One day he told them, "I have to return you to your people on Earth. Your fathers will have to remain here. Once you get into Heaven you can not return to Earth." He opened up the floor where he was seated and they looked down and saw the Earth. This was the first time that they realized

111

they were actually in Heaven. The chief took the two boys and threw them through the hole.

The prince's son landed on a big fir tree or *saywx*, not far from his home village. The cousin's son landed on some kelp in the ocean. They were wrapped in beautiful blankets. The men practising archery used to shoot at the big tree to see how far the arrows would travel. When it had too many, they decided to cut the tree down in order to salvage the arrows. While they were collecting the arrows, one of them found the boy deep in the tree, wrapped up in a beautiful blanket. They were very surprised.

They took the boy back to the chief who was really his grandfather. The chief looked at him and was sure it was his grandson. He was very happy. But the boy would not eat. Soon after this, someone else in a village from another clan reported that he had found a boy on the water. He, however, began to eat right away and he grew up with the rest of the villagers.

The chief's grandson, however, would not eat. It did not seem to harm him. He grew very fast. The chief sent word to all the people that he wanted someone to try to feed him. A few days later, a big canoe came to the shore of the village. In the canoe were two big people wearing large hats. They were invited in right away and they were seated at the head of the table and fed.

While they were eating, one of the guests asked the chief if he could hold his grandson. The boy's guards observed something. The guest's legs were covered with scabs. He took a scab from his leg, put it inside the food that he had chewed and offered it to the little boy.

The boy opened his mouth and ate it. The chief was very happy. The boy kept on eating and so did the two guests. It so happened that children were playing on the shores of the ocean and they found that food was bubbling out of the earth. They took wooden pegs and plugged the holes. The guests suddenly stopped eating and they left. The boy went on eating. Soon he had eaten everything in the house. Then he had eaten everything in the village. The chief decided that he had to abandon the child. He would leave some food with him and leave. If the boy was clever enough he would manage to survive.

They left the boy. The chief sent out town criers to tell the villagers they had to move.

"Demloi get zel cheb,
Demloi get zel cheb."

Everyone packed and left the young man behind.

The young man found that it was very difficult to live. He ran out of food. But he could not stop eating so he started to wander. He came across a little house. In it lived a man and his wife and their house was full of food. He became their guest but the man would not allow him to be lazy. Every morning, they went out before dawn for halibut. It was always the same thing. The man sat in the bow of the canoe and *Weeget* sat in the stern.

They always had to return before the sun rose. One morning when their canoe was full of halibut, *Weeget*'s host said, "We have got to go back in. We have to get back before the sun comes up."

By this time, *Weeget* is sure he knows who the man is, so he cries, "No. We had better stay out here just a little bit longer. We are catching lots of halibut today. We should stay out just a little bit longer." Soon the sun started to rise and the man started to melt. He said to *Weeget*, "I am getting very warm and I am afraid." *Weeget* replied, "Don't worry. I will cover you up with the blanket and you won't be so warm." He pulled the blanket over him. Soon it was getting hot. The man melted. He was made of pitch and pitch ran all over the halibut. His host's name was *Quisken*.

Analogues

In *Raven Traveling*, as told by John Sky of Those-born-at-Skedans, there is reference to two big-bellied fellows who scratch themselves over the heart after a bath and then eat the scabs. Once the scabs have been swallowed, the resulting hunger cannot be satisfied.[1]

In his *Origin of TXÄ'MSEM* Boas also refers to the eating of scabs accompanied by insatiable hunger. In this story it is a "shining youth" who is forced to move on by his father, a chief, because he has eaten all the people's food.[2] In the Ken Harris story, the villagers are the ones who move.

Because the versions collected by Boas are Haida stories, they are part of a large corpora known as "The Raven Legend." Boas also found Tsimshian versions with a supernatural child, again Raven, refusing to eat, and thus worrying his parents or grandparents. This child is induced to swallow some scabs, becomes voracious, and is deserted.

Ken Harris remarks that *Weeget* is sometimes called *Trēnsem*, but says that he is never referred to as Raven except in the one story he tells above. Both *Weeget* and *Trēnsem* belong to the House of *Hagbegwatku*, and the Raven clan is not of this house.

Boas relates an almost identical story of the murder in *TXÄ'MSEM Kills Little Pitch*, with a different ending.[3] After Little Pitch has melted, Raven returns to the shore to look up Little Pitch's wife. House and wife have vanished, to be replaced by a little green spruce tree with a drop of pitch on one side. Then his canoe full of halibut disappears, to be replaced by a spruce log with roots. In all, Boas mentions nine versions of this story; of the Tsimshian, Tlingit, Haida, Nass, Rivers Inlet, Kwakiutl, and Comox. In three versions, Boas found that the murder of Pitch was connected with the story of the war against the Thunderbirds.

The pitch incident occupies a small part of the Ken Harris version. It is interesting to note, however, that melted pitch covers a Chief's young son in the beginning of the story, and that the melted *Quisken* or pitch ends the saga.

---

[1] Swanton, *Haida Texts*, p. 123.

[2] Boas, *Tsimshian Mythology*, pp. 58-60.

[3] Ibid., p. 86; notes, p. 683.

2.

Weeget and the Water

In the old days there was no water. The only source was found in the pockets of a little plant. But *Weeget* knew that there was a main source of water guarded by a woman. He went there one day and found the woman sleeping on top of the well. He woke her up and said, "Your friends are just down there a little way. They want to see you." She took one look at *Weeget* and said, "Get out of here, *Weeget*, we all know about you."

But *Weeget* was very persistent and he made a plan. He found some blackberries and he chewed them. He made them into something that looked like human excrement. He took it over to the woman, lifted her blanket and stuck it underneath.

He woke her up again and said, "I am telling you, you did something bad when you were sleeping. If you don't believe me, take a good look." She looked under her blanket and she was very surprised. She was embarrassed. She got up and ran into the bush.

When she had left, *Weeget* took a couple of big buckets of water from the well, one in each hand, and he started to run. Wherever he splashed some water a lake was formed. Finally, he was so tired he dumped the water. He dumped one to the right and one to the left. This is the source of the two rivers. The Nass River was out of the pail on his right and the Skeena River was out of the pail on his left.

115

Analogues

Weeget has many adventures. Ken Harris has included just this one in his present collection. It is important as it appears to be unique to the Nass and Skeena Rivers.

HOW THE PEOPLE OF *DAMELAHAMID* FIRST BROUGHT THEIR FORM OF CIVILIZATION TO THE QUEEN CHARLOTTE ISLANDS

This demonstrates the spread of the culture of the people of *Damela-hamid* to the Haida and shows also the origin of a pilgrimage chant sung as the boys returned to the mainland.

1.

The Strange Pregnancy

The Indian word in the oral myth translated as "knowing" a young girl makes specific reference to knowing her sexually.

Ken Harris says that the salmonberries on the Queen Charlotte Islands are different to those on the mainland. When one looks inside the berries on the Islands, one finds little pieces of fur. These were the mice that the young princess had inside her.

Many hundreds of years ago, there lived in *Damel-ahamid* a chief whose sister had married a chief from another clan. This couple had a daughter who was of marriageable age, but she was very fearful of taking a husband. She had a lot of suitors, but she did not want to be married. Many people from other villages came to ask her hand in marriage, but she would not accept anybody. This went on for a long time.

One night the daughter woke up and felt a tickle in her throat. It made her choke and she could not understand what it was. She told her parents in the morning but no one could understand what was the matter. Eventually, after a period of time, she began to appear pregnant. Her lower abdomen started to swell and she told her mother.

Her mother looked at her and came to the conclusion that she had seen somebody without the benefit of marriage. Every-one became very concerned because no one was allowed to bear children unless they were properly married.

They asked her if she had been seeing anyone and she answered "Definitely, No." They questioned all the servants.

The princess used to sleep on a balcony called *tyak tyak*. The only way to the balcony was by a ladder and usually servants slept at the bottom to guard the princess. No one could have access to the *tyak tyak* without the servants being aware of it. But the servants said that nobody had passed them. It was a very mysterious thing.

Over a period of time her father became overcome with shame. His young daughter was subject to the supreme penalty, death. He loved her so much that he tried everything before he made his decision.

He called all the suitors. He went into all the buildings where they lived and very thoughtfully asked them if anything had happened, if any of them had known his daughter. They all said, "No."

Finally he ordered his servants to make a great big box. They sealed it very tightly with pitch. It was a very special kind of pitch that was also used to seal the canoes. It did not harden and it did not melt. It was a special preparation.

The father lined the box with blankets associated with the House of *Hagbegwatku*. His daughter was *Hagbegwatku*'s grandniece. On the appointed day they put her in the box and took her out to the middle of the river and cut the box loose.

The box floated down the Skeena. The strange thing about it was that it did not catch on any of the sandbars. The box kept its course in the middle of the river.

The box drifted right to the mouth of the river. It then drifted across the Hecate Straits and finally landed on the point known as Rose Spit. There were people living on the Islands. It was the policy that the chief had to get up early in the morning and go about his daily routine. A young chief, who was not yet married, was up very early that morning and went to walk on the beach.

It was the custom that the chief had first claim to anything that landed on the beach. He knew that many times things would wash up on the point. He went to check the point. He saw something that appeared to be man-made. He couldn't see exactly what it was, but he did not get too close to it. He went back for his servants and told them to investigate. They did. When they came back, they told him, "It is definitely made by man. It is sealed and it has a cover which is also sealed tight."

He ordered his servants to take tools and open it gently. And they did. They opened it gently. They found in the box blankets and clothing belonging to a princess. A young girl was lying amid the blankets.

They all immediately knew that she was a princess of *Damelahamid* of the *Gisgahast* clan. The blankets had identified her with the house and her clan. The killer whale crest was also there.

The young chief was very pleased that he had found the box. At the bottom of the clothing was this young girl. They all looked at her and they realized what had happened because the laws of the people were the same everywhere. They knew that this young girl had been sentenced to death because she was pregnant without the benefit of a husband.

They took her into the chief's house and they brought in midwives. These women knew what they were doing. They examined the girl and then they came to the conclusion that she was not bearing a child. There was definitely something wrong with her, but she was not bearing a child.

The young girl would not eat. She just choked. So they called all the people, all the wise men, and they decided what they were going to do with her. They made their decision. They took all her clothes off and clothed her with something very thin. They took her down to the shore of the ocean and they submerged her in the water until she started to shiver. She got very, very cold.

The next thing you know is that her mouth opened and out of her mouth came a little mouse. And it was followed by other mice. It was a mother mouse with little baby mice. There were a total of twelve in all — one mother and eleven baby mice. They ran up the shore.

The people tried to catch them, but they were so fast that

they could not. They all disappeared into the salmonberry bushes.

All the people realized that after the mice had left her voluntarily, she became normal. She started to eat. The people continued to treat her and gave her medicine which cleaned her out thoroughly. She told them what had happened.

They took her in. The young chief decided that he was going to marry her. It was quite obvious that she had not disgraced herself. So they were married. The chief's mother was not too pleased because normally a wife was chosen carefully for the chief. However, the young girl was a princess of the House of *Hagbegwatku* of *Damelahamid*. It was felt, though, that since she had been cast off and rejected by her own people, she was not really fit to be a wife of the chief. However, her new clansmen did the right thing.

They took her and purified her in the manner that our people purify a disgraced person in their family. They decided that a gross error had been made and they purified her in the eyes of the people. And the young chief of the Haida took her for his wife. They lived for many years and they had children.

Analogues

Boas places his Tsimshian version soon after the Deluge, and he identifies the site as Prairie Town.[1] It adds a young man coming at night to lie with the Princess. She sees him transformed into a mouse who leaves through a knot-hole above her bed.

When his daughter is placed in the box, the chief adds ten costly coppers and many elk skins, marten blankets, and all kinds of expensive

---

[1] Boas, *Tsimshian Mythology*, p. 232; notes, pp. 747, 791.

garments. The chieftainess on the Queen Charlotte Islands who found the box had recently lost her young daughter. Mice escaped from the newly opened box. The princess marries the nephew of the person who found her and has four boys and two girls. This version concludes with a story that Ken has separated from it, but which follows here. The six children eventually leave in a canoe to find their mother's people who received them gladly. They all survived.

The bereft mother remaining on the Queen Charlotte Islands found her original mice children who taught her how to dance and sing, and she taught the rest of the people on the Islands.

2.

Return to Damelahamid

This story is another lesson in morals. Every time the law of the people is broken, they have to suffer the supreme penalty. The children in the canoe perished.

When the chief's children were growing up in the Queen Charlottes, they loved to play. They played outdoors and they played indoors and they never stopped playing. There was a large number of them. When they were all playing one of the boys accidentally bumped into their grandmother. She became very upset and in her anger she rebuked them all and said, "You children of unknown origin! You are so crazy! Why don't you just settle down!"

This was all the children needed to hear. They went to their mother, very upset and told her what their grandmother had said. She had told them that they were of unknown origin!

Their mother sat down and said, "I am going to tell you what happened." She told them the whole story right from the beginning. She told them that they came from the highest house of the *Gisgahast* clan in *Damelahamid*.

From that day on their only wish was to go back to *Damelahamid*. They wanted to go to their own city and meet their own relatives. They finally talked their father into preparing them for the journey. He had a big canoe built and he loaded it with provisions. He gave them a lot of shellfish. They then set out on their long journey.

They went up the Skeena river or the *Kshian*, and as soon as they could see parts of *Damelahamid* they became very excited. Two of them got out of the canoe and they started to pull it with a rope to make the journey faster. But the current was very bad and they had a problem controlling the canoe. It upset. Everyone in the canoe perished.

The two survivors managed to get to *Damelahamid*, and introduced themselves to the chief, and told him what had happened.

The chief told his people that the children of his daughter had returned. They were welcomed to *Damelahamid*.

The two survivors settled in *Damelahamid*. They told everyone of their journey from the Queen Charlotte Islands.

Conclusion

Ken Harris tells how his people have connected their lives with the telling of the Myths.

After *Skā twa*'s daughter was taken into Heaven, she bore three children. These children were returned to earth at *Damelahamid*. Their names were *Liggeyoan, Akagee* and *Goestella.* These were their names in Heaven. After they landed on earth, things happened. This is how our people created their titles. It is all related to some time in history when something really happened. Our people either create a chant or a lament; a chant relating to the actual happening.

After the three children were put on earth by their Father-in-Heaven, they evidenced the death of their relatives. During the battle when things got a little too rough for them, fog would set in and they would disappear. They would disappear in the fog and their opposition would slay each other in the fog. Names are born as a result of this.

You will recall that they brought a little gambling box with them from Heaven. They used this when they visited the village that had destroyed their ancestral village. It was the second oldest son who carried this box. *Akagee.* The box is known as *goldum tsean.* You will also recall that during the battle when an arrow would land, the little girl would pull the arrow out of their bodies and heal the wound with her hand. Another name was born again there. *Goestella*'s name on earth became *Tsim ham haemid* meaning "the healer." *Akagee*'s name became *Goldum tsean* because he was the custodian of the gambling box. *Liggeyoan*, who was the oldest of the three children, became known as *Hagbegwatku* because of the method they used to avoid fighting by becoming obscured in the fog.

They became very important in the formation of a new organization. *Hagbegwatku* became recognized as the first born of the nation and this is reflected in the seating arrangements in their houses. The elder or the first born, or the ruler of the house, sits right in the middle of the house at the end. At the back of the house he has a seat right underneath the roof joint and this is where *Hagbegwatku* sat. That was his seating arrangement. To his right is seated his brother *Goldum tsean.* These are traditional seating arrangements. I mention these two to illustrate the importance our people place on the origin of their civilization.

Tsim ham haemid, because she was the only girl, became the mother of this new nation. She became the matriarch of the *Gisgahasts.* They became *Gisgahasts* because of the little pole, the *gilhast,* they brought in their box, the *hawlhz-ganku.* They planted the *gilhast* outside their house and it grew. It was their first totem pole. It was the sign of their authority. So their nation became known as *Gisgahast* and *Tsim ham haemid* became their first Mother-on-earth. She became the matriarch. They adopted a matrilinear system because of *Tsim ham haemid.* Her children succeeded *Hagbegwatku.* Other names were created because of relationships with areas, with happenings and events.

Time passed. They settled in *Kitsekucla.* At this time it was told that *Hagbegwatku*'s son was married in Kitwanga and his wife was of the House of *Gogch.* She had two children. Their names were *Massanal* and *Demdelachu. Demdelachu* was the girl's name. It was told that these two youngsters became very much involved with each other and they committed the sin of *kaitz. Hagbegwatku* was very upset with this and chastised them and told them that they had to leave. They moved across to the other side of the river. After a while they were overcome with remorse and they decided to return to their grandfather who was known to be a very good man, a very forgiving type of person. They travelled to *Kitsekucla.* At this time there were a lot of people threatening wars. There were raiding parties

128

and people had to identify themselves before they could be brought into the village.

So, one day, on the opposite side of the river from *Kitsekucla*, their appeared two people. And they gave the word. They told the people that they would like to be brought across to *Kitsekucla*. The normal way was to identify themselves and identify with whom they were going to be guests. They identified themselves as *Massanal* and *Demdelachu* and they told the people that they were guests of the house of their grandfather *Hagbegwatku*. A runner was sent to *Hagbegwatku* and he was told that *Massanal* and *Demdelachu* were on the opposite side of the river and they were waiting to be carried across. The people by this time were very much aware of what had happened, and because of the nature of the circumstances, they had to be very careful of how they dealt with the two youngsters.

Hagbegwatku told them to bring the two across and he immediately sent out a messenger to call all his brothers and he called a council. When *Massanal* and *Demdelachu* were brought to the village of *Kitsekucla*, they were taken to *Hagbegwatku*'s house and he ordered his servants to lay out the table at the head of the house. By this time, some of his relatives had arrived. His brother *Goldum tsean* had already arrived and was seated beside him. When *Massanal* and *Demdelachu* were brought in at the door, he looked at them and *Hagbegwatku* looked at his brother and they were overcome. They were overcome with sorrow. They felt very sorry for their young grandson. He had confessed that he had done wrong and he was prepared to correct it. He had thrown himself at the mercy of *Hagbegwatku* and his brother *Goldum tsean*. So *Hagbegwatku* asked his brother, *Goldum tsean*, to move over to one side, and *Hagbegwatku* himself moved over to make room for their grandson at the Head of the House. They called *Massanal* and, true to the spirit of honouring guests, they seated him at the Head of the House where *Hagbegwatku* himself normally sat.

Hagbegwatku called a feast and he told the story to all his brothers who, out of respect for their chief, agreed that *Mas-*

129

sanal should be taken into the House and be treated as an honoured guest.

And *Shlagomlehagh*, another chief of the *Gisgahasts* took *Demdelachu* into his House and adopted her into his clan. The time passed, but the chiefs of the *Gisgahasts* were not very happy with what had happened. They kept their feelings to themselves. They were not in any position to dispute the decision of their chief, but they were very unhappy.

It came to pass that in *Kisgehas*, further up the river, there was a sickness in the House of *Weeget*, a chief from the *Gisgahasts*. This sickness was attributed to sorcery and witchcraft. The witch came to the house of *Weeget* and demanded great wealth in order to spare the life of one of *Weeget*'s subjects.

When they had given the witch a large amount of wealth, he also demanded that he be given a woman from the House of *Weeget*. This, too, was done. However, by this time the person was too ill and there wasn't anything that witchcraft could do to reverse the spell cast on him. It was too late. The person died. The woman given to the witch from the House of *Weeget* honoured the decision of the chief and went with the witch as his wife. However, she had made up her own mind that she was going to avenge her brother's death.

And it came to pass that in the middle of the winter she took a knife and, while her husband was sleeping, cut off his head. She took the head back to *Kitsekucla* because she was from the House of *Hagbegwatku* and she knew that *Hagbegwatku* was a wise chief with many answers. She carried the head to the people of *Kitsekucla* to show that she had done the honourable thing and had avenged the wrong that the witch, her husband, had inflicted on her family, and she was accepted.

Still the people were not very pleased with *Massanal*. They thought he had taken advantage of the goodwill of *Hagbegwatku* and his brothers. He remained as a guest. There were times when *Hagbegwatku* wanted to give him a title, but his brothers very seriously objected. They told *Hagbegwatku* that it was enough that he had corrected a wrong that had been done. They said, "It is enough that you love your grandchild. But there are things that you just cannot do and this is one of them."

It came to pass that *Massanal* died and he was succeeded by one of the children of his own sister, *Demdelachu*, who had been taken into the House of *Shlagomlehagh*. So *Demdelachu*'s child succeeded his uncle, but he was not given a name. He was called *Massanal*, the title that his uncle had.

The newcomer from *Kisgehas* felt very sad about this, and she made a plan. She accepted *Demdelachu* as her own sister and she passed on the name of *Weeget* to her adopted nephew who had succeeded *Massanal*.

Hagbegwatku also made a decision. He gave *Massanal* a *nochnoch*, a *nochnoch* that had been kept in his House for a long time. This was the Thunderbird, *Twe tjea-adku*. So *Massanal* received the name of *Weeget* and the *nochnoch*, *Twe tjea-adku*, and continued to live in *Kitsekucla*. *Massanal* occupied the first seat, the main seat in the centre of the House of *Hagbegwatku* and became the visitor who never left.

Glossary

PLACE NAMES

An twe lilbergue	located at what is now known as Butze Rapids
Dahemgeest	Lake of the Swans where the sisters of *Deelep-zeb* fished for trout
Da ochems	name of the man-made hill in *Lo-tres-kū*'s Story
Damelahamid	new and beautiful land described by grandfather or Father-in-Heaven to three children, *Liggeyoan*, *Akagee* and *Goestella*. He promised to place them in this land and told them to build their new home there. The present area known as *Damelahamid* is situated between the Nass and Skeena Rivers in the area near Hazelton.
Gisseku-la	a little river the six brothers travelled down on their return to *Damelahamid*. This became *Gissegucla* the river that flows from *Tje goeych we*.
Guljeb	a village
Kitsekucla	favourite hunting ground down the Skeena River from *Damelahamid*
Kisgehas	village up the river from *Kitsekucla*
Kshian	Skeena River
La Haidah	Queen Charlotte Islands
La Hein	Prince Rupert
Mean tse kho don	Seeley Lake, at the "Base of the Mountain"
Spanachnoch	a place where spirits or monsters are supposed to have lived until they were called upon
Spokehōd	now known as Port Essington, the place where the second *dakh* landed. The people of the coast, the Tsimshians, came from this *dakh* according to Ken Harris.
Stekyawden	now called Rocher Deboule, the big mountain overlooking Hazelton. Also called *Twe-tgoi-it tje*, or "Where I was frightened"

Tjai-elhz gegukla	mountain near Lake *Dahemgeest*
Tkan-Damelahamid	land that was made flat; it probably refers to the Prairie Provinces. Irene Harris had heard about this land since she was a little girl and later in life was very happy to have seen it on her way to Toronto.
Tse-lahad-hū	"Where ashes were spilt," a part of *Dahemgeest* Lake
Tselisam	Nass River
Twe-tgoi-it tje	"Where I was frightened," or Rocher Deboule
Weguljeb	any city, large in size or importance
Wintse hidku le loch	"the place where they got copper from"
Wissinskid	the mountain behind *Kispiox* where the first *dakh* landed

INDIAN WORDS

adelhz leeai	asking for pitch from a spruce tree
ad-hū	ashes. *Tse-lahad-hū* means "where ashes were spilt."
anuwish-ū	cloistered place where menstruant girls were segregated
ahk hkai-hō	sleigh or sled
chehū	excrement
dahemgeest	swan
dakh	house of logs: 12 logs on each end and on both sides
dakhumhast	house belonging to the pole or *hast*
daptlhz	spear
delhz	belt of mountain sheep's wool with fringe at the end
demloi get zel cheb	"everyone has to move."
eez	pocket
gelink	utility box
gidwinthu	northern woodpecker
gilhast	first totem pole. *gil* = prime, *hast* = pole.
gisgahast	people of the fireweed
givees lootsen gues	"make more room for himself"
goldum tsean	gambling box

133

guljeb	village
hae gae hesku	stone used to sharpen cutting tools
ha goelhz	skinning knife
ha-ut	pileated woodpecker
hawlhz-ganku	decorated magician's storage box
hegee	instrument for killing, similar to a tomahawk but much larger. There are very few of them left. The *hegee* in the story was the only one made in *Damelahamid*.
helhz le gyawku	axe for cutting trees
hlicht	term used for young people
kaitz	incestuous relationship
koelhz se mos	means "Small rock platform appear suddenly!"
lah ma-un	salt water
lan num ghide	ceremonial hat covered with ermine fur and abalone shell
loggum melhz tjalhz	feather shavings
lo gin a gwelk	"The bear was land-locked."
medeek	also *medeekum juwyax*; monster bear who lived in the land-locked lake
medeekum hatl wap	bear swimming in Hecate Strait adopted by *Lo-tres-kū*
melhuish	devil's club roots used in bath for decontamination rites
meshum la-up	little red stone
mess plong	albino sea-otter
mismah or *machmah*	hole in space leading to Heaven
Nalhzdum an nex cu tloeh goe / Dem an skā-twa-m	"If anybody is going to marry my granddaughter, please show yourself now."
nochnoch	a variety of spirit capable of taking on different human or animal forms. It is also descriptive of supernatural ability.
no-elhz	utensils, pots, pans, dishes
olhunku	rope of spruce roots
owenzeets	a *taboggan* with helpful powers
saywx	big fir tree
skan milkst	wood of wild crabapple tree used for handles of *helhz le gyawku*; still found in the Hazelton area
skan tsnaugh	type of tree used to make snowshoes. The berries on it are still called *tsnaugh*.

134

taboggan	little field mouse
tdek	ball made from stomach of a bear
tdo-a	invited guests
teeits	visitors who summon guests to a feast
tgadlech	carrying straps for storage box
tgoi	hood covering the head of a young girl in her first menstrual period
thwel-lahz	bags made of cedar bark for carrying water
tja-hō	baton. *Wīn tdek-hu tja-hō* means "Where the *tja-hō* was left"
tje goeych we	a sudden fright. *Twe-tgoi-it tje goeych we* means "Where I was frightened."
tse kho don	heart of mountain, becomes *Stekyawden*
tsuni	"oh, yes!"
twe-tgoi-it	a big hood
tyak tyak	an inside balcony area on which people sleep
weguljeb	a city, large in either size or importance
windottha	a drug prepared from the new top growth of poplars. It is mixed into a very hard paste like chewing gum and stuck in the mouth behind the teeth and it is said to give energy.
wintse hidku le loch	"The place where they got the copper from"
yon nelhz tle lo guenkū dum tsewen	defecate

PERSONAL NAMES

Irene Harris	c. 1888 - 1972. Born at Lorne Creek, B.C. and buried at Kitwanga. She had five titles.
Kenneth Harris	Born 1928. Has three titles.
Arthur McDames	1855 - 1962. Born at Lorne Creek, B.C. Buried at Kitsegucla. He had ten chief positions or titles.
Akagee	second-born son of the survivor of the battle on the Nass River after she entered Heaven
Awāk	chief of Haida people
Deelepzeb	means "His own city." A leading name, given to a prince who is destined to be the Chief of *Damelahamid*. This was Ken Harris's first title.

Demdelachu   daughter of *Hagbegwatku*'s sister, guilty of *kaitz* with her brother, later adopted by *Schlagomlehagh*

Ghuldeg Hed   chief of the Frog phratry, living across the river from *Damelahamid* where Hazelton is now located. He is called *Hed* for short.

Gid tse tgan   *Goesmessnech*'s servant

Gisgahast   People of the *hast* or the Fireweed people. There is an old Indian saying, "Fireweed grows like *Gisgahast*." It is found among all the Northwest Coast Indians. The Fireweed phratry is found among the Gitksan, Tsimshian, Nishga, Haida, Kwakiutl, Tlingit, Salikshan and the Wakashan.

Gitshian   also spelt *Gitksan*

Goesmessnech   Name of the large white killer whale

Goestella   third-born child, a daughter, of the survivor of the battle on the Nass River after she entered Heaven

Gooch nach no emgit   means "He is known throughout the World," the son of *Gudeloch*

Goodip hae gae hesku   fifth-born, a son, of young lady living in early *Damelahamid*; named after his mother's action of placing a stone used to sharpen cutting tools, a *hae gae hesku*, in the crease of her gown around her stomach

Goodip skan milkst   second-born, a son, of young lady living in early *Damelahamid*; named after his mother's action of placing shavings of *skan milkst* in the lining of her gown around her stomach

Goodip skan tsnaugh   third-born, a son, of young lady living in early *Damelahamid*; named after his mother's action of placing shavings of *skan tsnaugh* in the lining of her gown around her stomach

Goo ha goelhz   seventh-born, a daughter, of young lady living in early *Damelahamid*; named after her mother's action of placing a little skinning knife, *ha goelhz*, in the crease of her gown

Goldum tsean   Earth name of *Akagee*.

Goo loggum melhz tjalhz   sixth-born, a son, of young lady living in early *Damelahamid*; named after his mother's action of placing shavings from a feather, *loggum melhz tjalhz*, in the crease of her gown

Goo meshum la-up	fourth-born, a son, of young lady living in early *Damelahamid*; named after his mother's action of placing a little red stone, a *meshum la-up*, in her gown
Gudeloch	a *nochnoch* in the story of of the Origin of the Killer Whale
Hagbegwatku	means "First Born." His Heaven-name was *Liggeyoan*. This is the top title of all the clans.
Hanamok	speaker of the House of *Hagbegwatku*
Kaelhzhu	one of the biggest chiefs on the Nass River. It is told that only one family survived the second battle on the Nass. The chief took his family upstream when he saw disaster. The name *Kaelhzhu* was born after the time of *Skā twa*.
Liggeyoan	first-born, a son, of survivor of the battle on the Nass River after she entered Heaven
Lo-tres-kū	The mother, or matriarch, of the Ravens; originally a young Indian princess from Kitwanga
Massanal	son of *Hagbegwatku*'s sister, guilty of *kaitz* with *Demdelachu*; his successor of the same name was given the thunderbird as his *nochnoch* and became the Visitor Who Never Left.
Medeekum hatl wap	*Medeek* escorting *Lo-tres-kū*
Nagwa	brother of *Hagbegwatku*; he uses the rainbow as his personal "coat-of-arms"
Nege-elhz	sister of *Deelepzeb*
Noelhz	first-born, a son, of young lady living in early *Damelahamid*; named after his mother's action of wiping her nose and rubbing the mucus on her stomach
Quisken	means "pitch." He was an old halibut fisherman who took *Weeget* out in his boat.
Schlagomlehagh	Chief of the Gisgahasts who adopted *Demdelachu*
Siggite looks	sister of *Deelepzeb*
Simoigetdamla ha	Chief-in-Heaven or Father-in-Heaven
Skā twa	Grandmother, one of two female survivors of battle between first two villages on the Nass River. The name was taken from her cry asking for a husband for her grand-daughter.

137

Tsimdakh	the people who originated from the *dakhumhast*, the House of *Liggeyoan*
Tshā get she lā	niece of the chief who was one of the berry-picking party at *Mean tse kho don* or Seeley Lake. She was slain by the *Medeek*.
Tsim ham haemid	Earth-name for miraculous healer, otherwise known by her Heaven-name, *Goestella*
Tsim ohl	younger daughter of Chief-in-Heaven
Tso ech	warrior brother of *Tshā get she lā*
Twe-tgoi-it	an old woman six brothers met on their return to *Damelahamid*. It means "big head-cover" and comes from *tgoi* or hood worn over the head by young girls during their first menstrual period. These girls were not allowed to look at the sky.
Twe tjea-adku	Thunderbird
Way deetai	name of the stranger with light hair and very light brown eyes appearing in The Story of the Flood
Weeget	sometimes called *Trēnsem*. He was a mischievous being who had many adventures. Ken Harris stresses that he is not synonymous with Raven.
We tsim nossik	*Gudeloch*'s first wife, a wolverine and a *noch-noch* at the same time.
Yabadets	Warrior brother of *Tshā get she lā*. He and *Tso ech* killed the *Medeek*.

Major Sources

Franz Boas. *Tsimshian Mythology*. Washington, D.C.: Government Printing Office, 1916.

John R. Swanton. *Haida Texts and Myths*. Washington, D.C.: Government Printing Office, 1905.

Will Robinson (as told by Walter Wright). *Men of Medeek*. Kitimat: Northern Sentinel Press Ltd., 1962.

Viola E. Garfield and Paul S. Wingert. *The Tsimshian Indians and Their Arts*. Seattle: University of Washington Press, 1950.